SLAUGHTER UNDER TRUST

Glen

D1003737

CLAN DONALD COLLECTION

PER MARE · PER TERRAS

SLAUGHTER UNDER TRUST

Glencoe–1692

DONALD J. MACDONALD

Foreword by

Dr. I. F. Grant, M.B.E.

ILLUSTRATED
AND WITH MAPS

Delaware Free Press
Greenville, Delaware
U.S.A.

Library of Congress Catalog Card Number: 82-71642

Cover
Ranald Macdonald, 5 Kemble House, 58 Dean Street
London W1, England

Back Cover
Photo by permission of Miss Barbara Fairweather,
The Glencoe and North Lorn Folk Museum

Contents

Illustrations

LINE DRAWINGS

Acknowledgements

I should like to acknowledge with gratitude the generous help given me by Dr. I. F. Grant, M.B.E., LLD.: Sir William. Arbuckle, K.B.E., C.B., F.R.S.E.: Sir Iain Moncreiffe of that Ilk, Albany Herald: Dr. C. W. Graham: Noel Cook Esq.: Mrs. J. MacDonald Clarke: and Miss Dickson and her staff of the Edinburgh Public Library.

I am grateful to all who have helped me with illustrations and particularly to the following: The Earl of Stair and Lady Marjorie Dalrymple for the picture of the Master of Stair (later 1st Earl); the Duke of Buccleugh and the Duke of Argyll for the 10th Earl of Argyll (later 1st Duke); to Sir John Clerk of Penicuik, Bart., for The Highland Wedding; and to G. R. Harvey Esq. of Edinburgh for the drawings and map.

ENVOI

THE author is happy that this work has merited a reprint. The first edition was very well received and was adjudged to be a fair representation of the facts of history, unbiased, although written by a Macdonald. This opinion was still further confirmed by none other than the late Duke of Argyll when the author met him in Canada.

Much has been written about the tragedy of so long ago; but it is nice to know an annual service of remembrance is held at the Memorial Cairn in the Glen. For some years a mysterious floral tribute was found there on the morning of February the 13th annually. It had been laid by an old gentleman, Donald MacDonald, a descendant of one of the victims of the Tragedy of 1692. When this suddenly ceased owing to the death of old Donald, the Clan Donald Societies of Edinburgh, Glasgow and Aberdeen took up the torch to be joined later by those of Canada, USA, Australia and New Zealand. Now each year on the Day a company of clansfolk of Clan Donald, with others, is piped up to the Cairn. A service is held by the Rector of Glencoe and Ballachulish, and a lone piper plays the beautiful pibroch "Mort-Glinne Chomhainn." The wreath bears only the name of the presenting country of that year and the one word "CUIMHNICH" (remember). The service is one of remembrance, not of hate or vindictiveness.

The author now resides happily in old age on a half acre of land near the lands of The Armadale Clan Donald Centre, looking over the Sound of Sleat to Morar and Knoydart, with the Prince's Island in Loch Nevis. Here so many memories of the past come to his mind; and he has so many kind friends who call or write, that he can never feel lonely—he feels that he is of all men the most fortunate in that his wife, who has shared his life for 50 years, is still with him.

One last word: The author can never forget the kindness of his friends, Mr. and Mrs. Ellice McDonald, Jr. of Invergarry, Montchanin, Delaware, of which the financing of this reprint is only one, albeit the most recent.

Dundonald
Sleat, Isle of Skye
1982

DONALD J. MACDONALD
OF CASTLETON

Foreword

THE author of this book, Donald J. Macdonald, is a man dedicated to the service of his Clan. His direct ancestor, Macdonald of Castleton, took a leading part in the resounding Highland victory of Killiecrankie. For years he has laboured to keep alive among his fellow clansmen the memory of the old traditions and feelings of kinship that are the life-blood of a clan. He is thus well equipped to trace out the story of the long struggle between the Macdonalds and the Campbells which was so largely responsible for the tragedy of Glencoe.

The story of the Massacre is one of the few widely known incidents in Highland history. It had, of course, direct political repercussions, but I would venture to suggest that its influence has been even more pervasive. It is but one among many outrages committed against the people of the Highlands; but it was the first to arouse widespread and strongly felt condemnation. During the following two and a half centuries there has been a gradual but profound change in the general attitude towards the Highlanders. Before then they were virtually unknown to most Englishmen and were despised and disliked by their Lowland fellow-countrymen. The records of the Scots Privy Council make the attitude of the Establishment only too plain. The Lowland poets, the *makars*, only alluded to them in a few satirical phrases. Little did they think that a time would come when the kilt would be regarded as the national dress of Scotland and her national music that of the Highland bagpipe.

Hugh Macdonald, a clan historian, writing of the Battle of Harlaw, remarked that Macdonald had the victory but the governor the printer. From the end of the seventeenth century onwards, however, a host of writers has brought about a truer appreciation of Gaeldom. Their themes are not "success stories" but those of relentless tragedies and of these the Massacre of Glencoe is among the greatest.

I. F. GRANT

PUBLISHER'S COMMENTS

THE republication of SLAUGHTER UNDER TRUST in paperback is of particular interest to me on two counts.

First, my grandfather was born in Glencoe 139 years after the massacre and I am quite sure my forefathers were living in the Glen on that bitter winter morning of 13 February 1692.

As you may know this small but ancient branch of Clan Donald was founded by Iain Fraoch natural son of Angus Og, an historical fact which my wife pointedly brings up when she is irritated. Of course the Hendersons were in the Glen first but their male line ran out and the Chief's daughter married Iain Fraoch so Henderson and MacDonald blood were amicably joined under the name of MacIain.

On the second count my interest is stirred by the author himself, Donald J. Macdonald of Castleton, scholar, soldier, gentleman and one of the greatest clansmen living today. Throughout the years he has worked indefatigably to hold the Clan together and promote its best interests. If republication of this volume in the slightest degree enhances the prestige of this modest gentleman, if one out of one hundred readers come to realize what he has done for Clan Donald and the other Western Highland clans, then it has been worthwhile.

Invergarry   ELLICE McDONALD, JR.
Montchanin, Delaware
1982

Chapter One

THE GLEN AND ITS PEOPLE

GLENCOE is probably the best known glen in all the Highlands of Scotland, not alone for its scenic grandeur though that is unsurpassed in almost any country, but also for its fame as the scene of one of the saddest events in Scottish history.

The derivations of the name have been many and various over the years. In the fourteenth century it was spelt Glenchomure (Gleann a' Chomaire—the Glen of the confluence). In the fifteenth it became Glencole (Gleann Caol—the narrow glen). By 1500 we find it spelt Glencowyn and Glencoyne, in 1623 Glencoan, all meaning the narrow glen, and very aptly. In more modern times it becomes Gleann Chumhann, another spelling for the narrow glen. How names change! They always suffer badly in the transition from the Gaelic to Lallans or English languages. Since the Massacre some have tried to derive its name from the word *cumbach* meaning sorrow or weeping; but suitable as it might have been in 1692 or now, it is not the original name.

Approaching the head of the Glen from the south across the lonely Moor of Rannoch round the base of Buachaille Mor Eite (The Great Herdsman of Etive) one enters the glen on the watershed a mile from the cottage of Allt na Feadh at a height of 1,000 feet. From this point on the scene is one of beauty, savage and cruel in winter storms, or peaceful in summer heat, as the River Coe plunges down the defile towards the sea. To the north the long wall of Aonach Eagach (The Notched One) divides it from the sea in Loch Leven, while to the south the giant Bidean nam Bian with its spurs—Beinn Fhada (Long Mountain), Aonach Dubh (The Black One), and Stob Coire nan Lochan (Peak of the Corry of the

Lochs)—cuts off the low winter sun. Bidean nam Bian has
been explained as Peak of the Hides, and there may be a
reason for that name; but more simply it might as well be
derived from Bidean nam Beann, the Summit Peak of the
Mountains, which it certainly is—the highest peak of that
massif bounded by Loch Leven, Loch Etive and the Moor of
Rannoch. About half way down the narrowest part the
shoulder of Aonach Dubh seems almost to close in on the
road; and at that point high up on the rock-face a deep vertical
fissure marks what is called "Ossian's Cave". It is doubtful if
Ossian ever came here let alone could have lived in such a
cave. It was first entered within recorded history by a shepherd, Nicol Marquis, in 1868, when the floor which slopes up
at an angle of 45 degrees was covered with vegetation. Today
it is so often climbed that there is a visitors' book in a tin-box
for those who enter to sign their names! But there is a much
more romantic and celestial story about the cave and its
origin.

Before St. Fintan Mundus came to Glencoe and founded his
oratory on the Isle of Munde at the mouth of the glen, St.
Kenneth passed this way. He was a Pict of Co. Derry and
came on a missionary journey to Alba a year before Columba
came to Iona. He has left his name in many places in Galloway, Kintyre and Argyll. Passing through on his way to the
East he made for Fife and shared with St. Serf the credit of
being the "Apostle" of Fife. But here in Glencoe he dwelt in
"a sunless place under a great mountain". One day, while at
his daily devotions, an angel appeared and offered to remove
the mountain and let in the sunlight! Kenneth declined the
offer; but the angel was not to be put off and made a start.
At last Kenneth persuaded him to stop—mercifully, for it was
hardly the task for a single angel. Probably the angel was
glad to desist; but he did not do badly to get as far as he did
into the rocky face! Kenneth returned eventually to Achadh
nam Bo in Ireland, and received the last offices at his death
from Fintan-Mundus, who then came over to Scotland (Alba
at that time) in 597, the year of the death of Columba.

The buttress of Aonach Dubh is sometimes called the
"Study" by a foolish mistake. This is of course a corruption
of the word *Stithy*, a Lowland word meaning "Anvil", a

translation from the Gaelic of An t-Innean, its proper name.

Just below this point the Glen begins to open out and at Loch Triachatan is the first inhabited site below the watershed. Here was the hamlet of Achadh Triachatan held by one of the cadet families of the Clann Iain. The river flows for a mile westwards and turns northward for three miles to the mouth of the glen at Loch Leven. This is the more fertile part and where most of the people lived. It is pleasant and sunny, open to the south over the shoulders of Aonach Dubh na Glinne and Meall Mor. To the north-east Aonach Eagach continues to dominate with its peak of Sgor nam Fiannaidh (The Rocky peak of the Fianna), and ending with its last bastion the well-known Pap of Glencoe (Sgorr na Ciche), overlooking the loch and the peaks of Mamore on the other side.

Sgorr nam Fiannaidh reminds one that, while the Fenians may not have come here, at least we may safely assume Deirdre and the sons of Uisneach must have known it well in their hunting expeditions from Glen Etive, where Deirdre built her "first home", after their flight from Ireland and the wrath of the King! In nearby Appin is the vitrified fort of Beregonium, better known in Gaelic as Dun Mac Uianich, the Fort of the Sons of Uisneach. Deirdre's tragic "Farewell to Alba" mentions with sad longing Gleann Eite amongst other glens of the west. She knew she was on her last journey!

Where the river turns north the Signal Rock above the farmhouse of Achnacon (Field of the hounds) looks up the Glen to the watershed, down to Carnoch at the mouth and up the Gleann na Lice Buidhe south-west where MacIain had a farmhouse, in which, according to some accounts, he was living at the time of his death in February 1692 (see pages 94–5). A beacon lit on the Signal Rock could have warned the whole glen of the call to arms.

From Achnacon and the Signal Rock to the sea the glen has a good stretch of arable land and woodland, with the townships of Achnacon, Inneriggan (Inbhir an Fheadhainn) and Carnoch (the present village of Glencoe) and in the neighbouring glen of Larach were more of the MacIains. Beyond Ballachulish (Baile a' Chaolais), the town of the strait, lie the lands of the Stewarts of Appin. Across the Loch are the lands of the Camerons of Mamore (later, Campbells). From Kinlochleven the MacIains' lands march with the Camerons east to the Moor of Rannoch, thence to the head of Glen Etive and down to Dalness, where the descendants of Ian Dubh held lands as cadets of MacIain. The line then returns across the summits of Beinn Maol Chaluim and Sgorr na h-Ulaidh to the Larach glen and Ballachulish.

Frontiers were of course somewhat fluid, but the Glencoe men were fortunate in that the natural barriers of the mountains were pretty definite and attacks of raiders could be easily forecast and dealt with. These same natural barriers were of course a disadvantage when it came to treachery within their very homes! And well the schemers knew it.

Thus the neighbours of the Glencoe folk were Camerons to the north, friendly, Stewarts of Appin to the west, also friendly for the most part, and South, but fortunately across the wild Moor of Rannoch, the Campbells of Glenorchy (later Breadalbane); and the less said about their relations with the MacIains the better—just at present.

Where the Camerons, Campbells and MacIains met on Rannoch is now the meeting place of the counties of Argyll, Inverness and Perth and the boundary post would have to be in the middle of a loch—Loch a' Chlaidheimh—the Loch of the Sword. The tradition is that the Chiefs of Glencoe, Lochiel, and Glenorchy met to fix the frontier at this spot, and having reached agreement each threw a sword into the loch to seal the bargain! Each had a strong party or "tail" in hiding near by, of course; but their swords were not needed. It is not to be supposed that the chiefs threw their best swords into the loch. A good Andrea Ferrara was too good to dispose of lightly!

In Loch Leven the Burial Isle, Eilean nam Marbh, or Eilean Munde, is a holy place, sanctified by the early Christian saint, Fintan-Mundus. Small islands like this are always popular as burial places in the Highlands; and this one is no exception, being shared by the Camerons and Stewarts with the MacIains. The enclosure of the MacIains is well marked, and funerals still cross to the isle, though not so frequently as in the old days. Like other burial isles it is said to be haunted by the spirit of the latest soul to be carried there, whose task it is to guard the graves until the next one arrives! Sometimes one of them has a very long vigil if the next funeral is delayed at all.

The saint who gave his name to the island was of noble birth, a relative of St. Columba. His mother was Feidelmia of the race of Maine, whence his second name. It is said that Fintan's father, Tailchen, came to Iona with the young Fintan, to be enrolled as a monk there. The boy returned to Eire and studied at Bangor and Cluain-Innis, and returned to Iona after Columba's death. In his journeys through Argyll he left his name in many places. There are several Kilmuns (Cille Munnu) but the best-known is that on the Holy Loch where his "baculus" or staff was kept for long. It was a holy spot and a resort of pilgrims. There are other pilgrims there now! Fintan resisted the Roman innovators, and adhered to the old Celtic practice. An old Irish writer called him "The torch with the ascending flame, Fintan, pre-tested gold, powerful, etc." Such was the saint who gave his name not only to the isle but to the old parish which used to cover both sides of Loch Leven and was called Eileanmunde.

This then was the territory of the Macdonalds of Glencoe, the smallest of the branches of Clan Donald, and the victims of the infamous massacre so well known in history. To understand to the full the events of 5 a.m. on the morning of the 13th February 1692 one must go back into history. The roots from which the Clann Iain sprang, their struggles for existence and their way of life have an important bearing on the attitude of their neighbours and the Government towards them, as well as their own sentiments and behaviour.

The founder of the family of the Chiefs of Glencoe was Ian Òg Fhraoich, Young John of the Heather, sometimes called Ian Òg Abrach because he was fostered in Lochaber. It is possible he was fostered in Glencoe among the people of his mother's clan. The practice of fosterage was important as it brought together all ranks of the Clan society. Dr. I. F. Grant says in her *Highland Folk Ways*, "Although it has long been obsolete (the latest example I have heard of was in the early eighteenth century) the old Gaelic custom of fosterage, the entrusting by men of position of one of their children to the care of an adherent, is an example of the close connection

2

between all ranks of society. Stories of the devotion of the foster-parents to their 'dalt' are among the most beautiful of Highland Tales." Young John was a natural son of Angus Òg of Islay, Lord of the Isles, by a daughter of Dugall MacEanruig (MacHenry or Henderson), the "chief man of Glencoe" to quote Mac Mhuirich and Hugh Macdonald, the historians of Clan Donald. Angus Òg was the "Lord of the Isles" who befriended Robert Bruce in his adversity and took some 5,000 or more Islesmen to the Battle of Bannockburn. When Bruce ascended the throne he did not forget his friend. The lands which had belonged to the MacDugall branch of Somerled's line were forfeited and with others bestowed upon Angus Òg. Among these were the lands of Glencoe, and he gave them to his son, Young John. Later, they appear in more than one charter from the Crown to John, Lord of the Isles, brother of Young John, who remained in peaceful possession until his death in 1358. He died in Knapdale and his body was taken to Iona and laid to rest beside his father's. Few of the stones of Clan Donald are now to be seen there; but that of Angus Òg of Isla lies in a penthouse to protect it from the weather. The site of the grave is unknown.

From the time of the founder the Chiefs are variously named Ian Òg, Ian Òg Abrach, or MacIain Òg Abraich; but they all seem to have borne the name, John, until the father of the Chief of 1692, who was called Alasdair, thus breaking the long line of Johns. Was this an omen? The varied fortunes of different names in a family would seem to be an interesting study. The *seannachies* seem to have been unable to sort out how many Johns ruled the Clan between 1358 and 1692. Records, written or otherwise, are scanty. The warriors of Glencoe appear in history only when engaged in the congenial occupation of raiding and plundering, often very far from home, not so often too near their fastness. One must not suppose, however, that the MacIains, any more than other Clans, spent all their time in raids and forays. So much is written about clan battles and feuds that casual readers of Highland history may be forgiven if they assume that the daily life of the clansmen was one of violence and freebooting. In fact, so long as their herds were safe and their crops fruitful they lived in peace; but times of famine would of course drive them to sterner measures to keep their wives and children fed. For the most part the disturbances of their peace came from outside their Glen. These were the quarrels of feudal superiors, the turbulent days of regencies, the rivalry of Covenanter and Episcopalian, and the fall of the Stewarts with the consequent rise of Jacobitism. All these evils followed the fall of the Lordship of the Isles, when Glencoe had fallen into the hands of feudal lords. The idea of feudalism was alien to the Gaelic spirit; and the attempts to force it upon the clans were the source of much strife.

Several exploits by the men of Glencoe come to light in the scanty records of the past. In 1501 they executed a spectacular feat of arms which has been described as "Fenian" by the Gaelic historians. That is to say it was worthy to be compared with the epic deeds of the Fianna of Ossianic times. A later Angus Òg, Master of the Isles, son of the last Lord of the Isles, John, who had been forfeited in 1492, had a son, Donald Dubh. This Donald, heir presumptive to the Lordship, was Angus Òg's son by a daughter of the Earl of Argyll. The threat of having a living heir to the Lordship was so dangerous to Argyll's plans that a kidnapping was arranged through the agency of Atholl. Argyll preferred someone else to do the dirty work. In addition he threw doubts upon the legitimacy of both Angus Òg and Donald Dubh, although the latter was his own grandson! So Donald was seized and imprisoned in the fortress of Inchconnel on Lochaweside for twenty-two years. At last, the men of Glencoe, whose loyalty to their patriarchical head was stronger than their obedience to any feudal superior, made a rapid march for more than twenty miles through enemy country, stormed Inchconnel and set Donald free, who of course at once set about trying to regain his lawful possessions. He was taken prisoner again and thrown into Edinburgh Castle. Once more he escaped and gave the regency much trouble until he died in Ireland in 1545. The MacIains certainly knew their way about Argyll, a knowledge that was to be very useful to Montrose later.

Another bold and skilful expedition was carried out by them in 1591. This time strange to say they did it at the behest of Argyll himself! He acted through the medium of

Campbell of Glenorchy, a cadet of the leading Campbell House of Argyll, who since 1563 held his lands, which included those of Glencoe. from the Crown. MacIain held Glencoe from Glenorchy in manrent with an undertaking to serve him against all persons save only the Authority itself (the Crown) and "my Lord Argyll". In 1591 a quarrel arose between the Ogilvies of Glenisla and Argyll. At a wedding there Campbell of Persie, an invited guest, insulted the bride and stabbed her father. Lord Ogilvy with difficulty prevented Campbell being killed, but he was expelled from the district with indignity. Argyll determined to avenge his kinsman; and mustered the Clann Iain with some others to invade the Ogilvy country and ravage it. The raid was carried out with speed and efficiency. Lord Ogilvy, his wife and bairns were themselves in danger, but escaped. A considerable spoil in goods and cattle was taken. In fact it was a most convenient arrangement for all except the Ogilvies. Argyll got his revenge and the raiders got replenishment of their herds and larders. The Government would issue the usual summons to the perpetrators to appear and answer for their misdeeds. They would not appear, would be "put to the horn" *in absentia* and no one would do much more about it! And so it turned out. Argyll was cited, failed to appear and was denounced as a rebel. By the end of the year the MacIains and others were "relaxed from the horn". It says much for the strangely disturbed state of Scotland, even in what are regarded as the more civilized parts, that a strong party of reivers was able to travel some 130 miles across the country, attack an estate and carry off their spoil back home without encountering serious opposition.

From this time until the Wars of Montrose in 1645 not much is known about their doings. They seemed to have lived in peace except for one regrettable incident when Alasdair MacIain Oig, possibly the brother of the Chief, was concerned in the murder of John Stewart of Acharn and another Stewart in Appin. It is very doubtful if Alasdair had the connivance or blessing of his Chief in thus disturbing the peace so near home. At any rate, after being imprisoned in Edinburgh for some time, Alasdair disappears from the records, so one may assume he paid for his actions.

In 1640 some of them were concerned with the Keppoch Macdonalds in a raid to the south. On their way home some of the Campbells of Lochtayside tried to exact more than the customary toll on a *creach* passing through their lands. A battle was fought at Stronachlachan in Glenlochay in which the Chief of Keppoch, Angus MacRaonuill Oig was slain. The Macdonalds seem to have got their booty away after killing eighteen of the Campbell gentry. In this fight the famous Ian Lom, the Keppoch bard, lost his father, a fact which did not make him love the Campbells. His poems thereafter are full of bitter satire and hate, which caused Argyll to offer, according to tradition, a handsome reward for his arrest.

In December 1644 a Glencoe man, Angus Mac Ailein Duibh, led Montrose and Alasdair Cholla Chiotaich (Young Colkitto, the most famous of all the warriors of Clan Donald) through the trackless wastes into the Campbell lands and as far as Inveraray. Angus promised Montrose good feeding for his men and well he kept his promise. The MacIains were out with Montrose in full force, and no doubt enjoyed their outing; but it did not increase the friendship between the two clans. If there ever had been any mutual regard, the raid on Inveraray destroyed it completely.

We come now to times nearer the events of 1692; and have followed the history of the Clann Iain as faithfully as we can with the scanty details available. Many factors work together to explain the restless lives of the clansmen of Glencoe.

After the secure occupation of their lands under the benevolent rule of their kinsmen, the Lords of the Isles, they found themselves the smallest of the branches of Clan Donald, isolated in an outpost far from their kinsfolk. The nearest were the MacDonells of Keppoch who lived in Brae Lochaber far over the mountains of Mamore and the Ben Nevis massif. They were surrounded by powerful neighbours, some friendly, others not so congenial. They lived in a small glen with a few acres and pasture of limited capacity for their cattle and flocks. It was the traditional duty of their Chief to provide the necessities of life for his children by whatever means he could find. Cattle-raiding was the obvious outlet for their activities, and the simplest solution to their problems. In addition it was in accordance with the best time-honoured customs of the Gael. The greatest epic of Gaeldom, the Tàin Bo Chuailgne (The Cattle Raid of Cooley) leading up to the Homeric exploits of Cuchullain and the warriors of Ulster, was founded on the cattle industry and the acquisition of wealth on the hoof from distant regions. It was always better to go far afield on these pleasant expeditions so as to avoid making bad neighbours. The "Tàin" was carried out all the way from Connacht to Ulster. Hugh, the first Chief of Sleat, celebrated his coming of age by raiding the Orkney Isles with great success, stopped off in the Gunn country of Sutherland on his way home, had a party and married the daughter of the local "crowner". The best territory for the western clans to raid was Moray. In 1645 Lochiel wrote to the Laird of Grant offering compensation for the action of some of his Clan in driving off cattle belonging to one of Grant's tenants whom they mistook for a Moray man "where all men take their prey". Of course getting the profits of the enterprise back home sometimes produced complications in the form of extra-mural overhead expenses. An accepted usage was that one should pay a tax, called the raiders' collop, to the clans through whose lands one passed. Naturally arguments were apt to arise, as no one had fixed a hard and fast levy on a percentage basis! A battle frequently ensued. Some of the Clans living along the Highland Line made a nice little profit by taking "protection money" from the Lowland farmers in their vicinity in return for guarding the passes by which the raiders came. Few of the Clans can point a finger at the Clann Iain for their cattle-lifting propensities. Most of them did it, some more often than others depending on their needs, and the necessity for extraneous food-supplies was nowhere greater than in Glencoe, where the population usually exceeded the ability of the land to support it.

Perhaps their most serious fault was the fact that they lived in the past and did not conform to the changes that had taken place in Scotland. The concept of feudalism and feudal superiors did not come easily to those accustomed to the old patriarchical system of the Lordship of the Isles. Neither Keppoch nor Glencoe held their lands by charter from the Crown; but their feudal lords got little joy from their superiority, and both miraculously kept possession of their estates down to the nineteenth century.

No doubt the men of Glencoe would have liked to live in peace, as indeed they did for long periods; but circumstances were against them. Their way of life, utterly essential to their very existence, did not endear them to their neighbours, nor to the powers of the Crown. Their sentiments were always out of date in the eyes of the Southron. They were hardy warriors, but still with their code of behaviour, rough and ready though it may have been. The fact that that code was ruthlessly violated in 1692 called forth the execration of all Highlanders. Even their enemies were appalled.

Chapter Two

ORIGINS OF THE MACIAINS (MACDONALDS) OF GLENCOE

THE Macdonalds of Glencoe, in common with all the other branches of Clan Donald, claim their descent from Somerled and the Lords of the Isles. The following brief account of that descent will explain why Macdonalds are proud of their ancestors. Dr. Grant in her book *Highland Folkways* gives a short account of the rise of the Highland clans. She writes: "Pride of place belongs to the clans descended from Somerled (who flourished in the twelfth century, the period when the feudalizing activities of the Scots kings were in full vigour). His name is Norse but the clan pedigree traces his descent back to Conn of the Hundred Battles, High King of Ireland. . . . About the earlier origin modern research is doubtful but it is highly important to remember that Somerled's descendants, the members of Clan Donald, strongly believed in this kingly descent." Somerled's line came down in males through his grandson, Donald eponymous of Clan Donald, and until 1354 were known as Rex Insularum, as legitimate successors to the ancient Viking kingdom of the Isles, an offshoot of the Kingdom of Norway, which Somerled had wrested from the Norsemen. He had no doubt about the strength of his position as his message to the King of Scots, when the latter laid claim to his landward possessions, shows. He said, "He had as good a right to the lands upon the continent as he had to the Isles. As to the Isles, he had an undoubted right to them, his predecessors being possessed of them by the good-will and consent of Eugenius the First, for obligations conferred upon him. When his forefathers were dispossessed of them by the invasions of the Danes (Vikings), they had no assistance to defend or recover them from the Danes; but

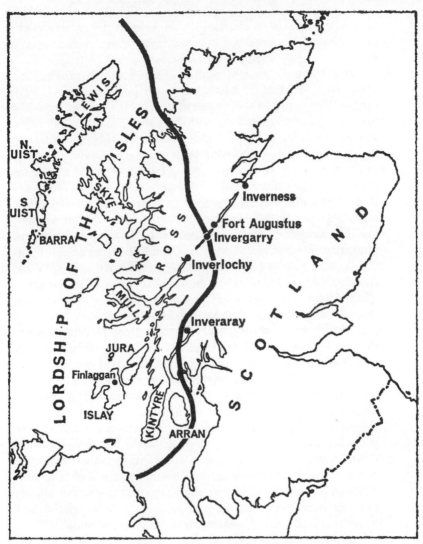

The Lordship of the Isles

however he would be assisting to the king in any other affairs; but as long as he breathed he would not condescend to resign any of his rights which he possessed to any."

After some division of Somerled's possessions among his sons when he died in 1164, all these lands and isles were united once more in the realm of John, fifth in line from the founder. John of Islay assumed the title of Lord of the Isles. It was not a feudal barony under the King of Scots, although the latter probably regarded it as such. It certainly did not function as such. The Lord of the Isles had his seat at Finlaggan in Islay which was a "manor-house" not a castle, and there he dwelt, moving around his domains from isle to isle and castle to castle. He gave charters to lands, kept a court, had his judges in each isle, and ruled like an independent potentate. He had his heralds too. Sir Iain Moncreiffe of that Ilk, himself now Albany Herald in Lyon Court, said, "While Macdonald was independent he had his own officers of arms. The MacLaverties were his hereditary heralds, or speakers, and it seems obvious that by the fifteenth century he had at least four proper officers: Islay Herald, Ross Herald, Kintyre Pursuivant, and Dingwall Pursuivant. These officers appear (otherwise inexplicably) on the Scottish Royal establishment immediately after the fall of the Lordship of the Isles. We can be pretty sure that his cadets, and other leading families within the Isles, would not have got away with the indiscriminate use of each other's rightful emblems, let alone the plain black galley on gold of Macdonald himself: the local Royal Arms. The Herald, or Pursuivant, is named after one of his master's attributes, and where he is called after a place it does not mean that he has duties in that place, but simply that his master is lord of it. The original coat of the first Macdonald and his successors was "Or, a galley sable". To this was added the red eagle, hung on the mast, for Ross; and the whole came to be surrounded by a royal tressure, either from descent from Robert II's daughter, or as a claim to local sovereignty. This coat was forfeited when the Lordship fell in 1493. In 1542, however, Lord Lyon Lindesay of the Mount recorded its memory under the heading "The Lord of ye Ilis" and shows a golden shield charged with a black galley and a red eagle behind the mast. This, then, is an authoritative record of the coat appropriate to whoever the Crown might recognize once again as the High Chief of Clan Donald."

After 1493 the various branches of Clan Donald and the other clans which had been within that confederation under the leadership of Macdonald became independent and went their various ways. But they never forgot their history and the ancient kingdom of the Isles held by their ancestors. The smallest and least powerful of these, the Macdonalds of Glencoe, were as proud of their descent as any of their more important kinsmen.

The clans thus formed were, in the chronological order in which they branched off the main stem, MacAlisters of Loup in Kintyre; MacIains of Ardnamurchan: MacIains of Glencoe: ClanRanald; Glengarry: Islay: Keppoch: and Sleat. The chiefs of these separate branches took their names usually from the founder of their families, but sometimes from a notable chief who followed him. They might also be referred to by the names of their estates. Thus the Chief of Glengarry could be called "Glengarry", "Mac 'Ic Alasdair", or "MacDonell of Glengarry". The Chief of Sleat is called in Gaelic "Mac-Dhòmhnaill nan Eilean". In English he is named "Macdonald of the Isles", "Macdonald of Sleat", or just "Sleat". "Clan-ranald", standing alone, may mean either the Clan or its Chief, according to the context: but there is no doubt about his Gaelic name—Mac 'Ic Ailein, the said Alan being the eldest son of Ranald, founder of this and also that of Glengarry through Alan's brother, Donald. The patronymic of Glengarry's chief, Mac 'Ic Alasdair, derives from the son of the said Donald. The Chief of Keppoch is known in Gaelic as Mac 'Ic Raghnaill (the son of the son of Ranald), although the founder of the family was Alasdair Carrach. Ranald was a notable later chief of that clan. Mac Iain of Ardnamurchan, Mac Iain of Glencoe, the Clan Godfrey and that of Islay are all called after their founders. The Chief of the Glencoe Macdonalds was referred to variously as MacIain, Glencoe, or Macdonald of Glencoe.

Generally speaking the simple name of the family, standing alone, always denoted the chief, e.g. Mackintosh, MacNab, etc. Where more than one clan bore the same name it was necessary to differentiate by adding their lands or territory, e.g. Macdonald of Glengarry, Grant of Glenmoriston, etc., although the spelling of the name might vary according to the preference of the different families. For example the Chief of Glengarry of 1660 adopted the spelling "MacDonell", a style used still among the Glengarry families. It should be noted that this accords more with the Gaelic original, provided the accent is on the "Don" and not the last syllable; for it is one of the great advantages of the Gaelic language that the accent falls always on the first syllable. Following this rule "Macdonald", standing alone, denotes the Chief of Clan Donald, Lord Macdonald, who was accorded this position by Lord Lyon in 1947, and the branches take the name of "Macdonald" followed by their territories. Here it is as well to note that now the practice has been adopted in some cases of prefixing the name of a chief by the article "The". It was not so of old, with one notable exception—The Chisholm (An t-Siosalach), one of whom was wont to remark that he alone, in company with The Devil and The Pope, was allowed to do this!

The Chief of the Campbells is known in Gaelic as Mac Chailein Mhòir, after Colin, their chief of the thirteenth century, who died in 1294 in battle. In English he is always known as Argyll after his Earldom, and there is little chance of any doubt about his identity. Breadalbane similarly is the name, and the only one apart from his Gaelic patronymic, used to denote that gentleman, again derived from his territorial Earldom. Before that creation he was simply "Glenurchy" or "Campbell of Glenurchy" from his territory before the expansion which later added to his domains.

The cadets of a clan were called by their family name followed by the name of their lands or farms, e.g. Macdonald of Achnacon. More often they were called simply by their lands as everyone at the time knew where those lands were and to which clan they belonged, although now it is necessary to refer to them by name as well, for clarity, as not everyone nowadays knows where the lands were or to which clan they belonged.

As we have said, at the fall of the Lordship of the Isles the branches of Clan Donald went their various ways although for a hundred years there were sporadic efforts to reinstate the old order. The result of this was that all the clans which had been in the Lordship still clung to their love of independence. Most sought and obtained charters to their lands from the King of Scots; but two refused to do so. These were Keppoch and Glencoe. This was the great stumbling block in the way of settling the Highlands peaceably. Misguided kings thought that by placing the clans under powerful feudal superiors— notably Argyll and Huntly (the chief of the Gordons) they would be kept in order. The Gael did not understand the feudal system, and did not want to. The old régime was his age-old way of life. The clan was a family, the chief the father, and all the members of the clan regarded themselves as children of one family and as good as any of the gentry. The chief ruled by consent of the clan; and in some cases could be changed by the clan if they did not deem him a fit person to lead them. He had to be capable of planning their well-being and leading them in battle. In the ClanRanald, which was always steeped in the old tradition, two chiefs were deposed and others put in their place when the clan thought them unfit to rule. One was actually assassinated, a very rare occurrence in any clan. He must have been a very bad man indeed. These customs were quite at variance with the feudal system with its superiors and serfs. The Gaels were never serfs. That unenviable status was an invention of the Anglo-Saxons and feudal Normans. As we shall see, if the Kings of Scots had only realized the attitude of the Gaelic clans and made them render allegiance to the Crown direct, without the intermediary superiors who were mostly foreign in the eyes of the Gael, or worse still fellow Gaels, like the Campbells, turned into part-Gael part-Saxon overlords, some peaceful settlement might have been arrived at. James V was perhaps the only monarch who tried to understand the Gael and he did have some success as the intense loyalty of the clans to the later Stewart kings witnesses.

Chapter Three

BEGINNINGS OF HATE

FOLLOWING on from the earlier history which has its bearing on the manner in which the Massacre was planned and carried out, we come to times nearer the event. In the minds of many the Massacre of Glencoe was the result of a clan feud in which all the Macdonalds were slain by the Campbells; and surprise is often shown that any Macdonalds are still alive. Between this extreme ignorance and the facts, there are many different opinions, most of them far from accurate. It is true that the deep-rooted hatred between the two clans had a great influence on the manner in which the massacre was carried out and especially in the choice of the tools to be employed. It may be as well to inquire how this enmity arose in the first place, and how it came to be fostered and increased as time went on. To do this we must look into history, briefly, and examine the rise of the Campbells to power, their methods and how these affected their neighbours. These forces gathered momentum as the seventeenth century opened; and, as that period proceeded, enmity and jealousy increased, breaking out into open warfare frequently. The political and religious developments in Scotland contributed to aiding the Campbells in their schemes, while at the same time militating against Clan Donald and similar clans. With the exception of a few smaller clans whose lands were too uncomfortably near Campbell territory for them to do other than support their powerful neighbours, the Highlands and Isles were divided into two factions—pro- and contra-Campbell. To this day these differences exist, even if in most cases they are a subject for jest.

In 1306 the newly crowned King of Scots, Robert Bruce, was in dire straits, and his adventures culminating in the

victory of Bannockburn and his firm settlement on the throne
are well known. In his adversity a few befriended him.
Amongst these were Macdonald and Campbell, the Chiefs of
their respective tribes or clans. Macdonald helped him in his
capacity as prince of a neighbouring realm: Campbell as a
feudal baron and vassal of his King.

While the Campbells have a long pedigree going back to
Diarmaid of Fingalian times, for the purpose of this book we
start with Gilleasbuig (Archibald) who became Laird of
Lochow by his marriage with Eva, heiress of Paul O'Duibhne,
from whom the Campbells are frequently known in Gaelic as
"Na Duibhnich". Their son, Cailean Mòr, became the first
knight of Lochow in 1280 under Alexander III of Scotland.
It is from him the Chiefs of Clan Campbell get their patronymic "Mac Chailein Mhòir". Colin was one of the forty
nominees to support Robert Bruce's father's claim to the
throne; but did not live to see that claim substantiated as he
fell in battle at Ath Dearg (Red Ford) in Lorne in 1294. His
son, Neil, second knight of Lochow, was Bruce's friend. After
his coronation in 1306 misfortune speedily befell Bruce. The
disastrous defeat at Methven and his all but fatal encounter
with the MacDugalls at Dalry in Lorne, where the famous
brooch of Lorne was lost, falling into the hands of the Mac-
dougal family who have it still, forced the King to flee with a
few faithful followers to the West. Sir Neil with Lennox
guided him through Lochlomondside into Kintyre where he
was received with every possible kindness and hospitality by
Angus Òg of Islay at his castles of Saddell and Dunaverty.
Later he was sent for safety to the Isle of Rathlin, still under
the protection of the Prince of the Isles, for the name Lord of
the Isles had not yet come into use, and the Lordship had not
been set up. From Somerled to Angus Òg the Chiefs of Clann
Cholla (the old name) were called Kings of the Isles (Rex
Insularum). Sir Walter Scott anticipated the Lordship in his
famous poem on this subject.

Sir Neil lived to fight at Bannockburn and see his friend
firmly seated on the throne. Angus Òg brought 5000 Islesmen to that battle, and fought in the centre under Bruce himself, who is said to have addressed him in the words "My
hope is constant in thee!" and these words are still used as a

motto by the Clanranald branch of Clan Donald. Sir Neil
died only two years later; but from that time the fortunes of
the Campbells were closely linked with the Crown of Scotland. They were vassals of the King; and, by careful cultiva-
tion of royal favours, skilful use of the law of the land, and
strategic marriages, they flourished exceedingly. Mac
Chailein Mòir was able to enjoy all the advantages of being
a feudal baron while at the same time exercising great power
as Gaelic Chief of a large clan with many confederates—a
clan which expanded all the time by the absorption of the
smaller clans adjacent to this territory. His geographical
position placed him as an ideal go-between for the King to use
in his efforts to pacify and absorb the Gaels of the western
seaboard and isles. Frequently the old excuse of "preserving
law and order" under a mandate from the Crown led to the
increase of power and lands in the hands of Mac Chailein
Mhòir! That potent chief seldom put a foot wrong; and even
if he did, as we have seen he did in the case of the raid on
Ogilvy, he was powerful enough to retreat to his fastness in
Inveraray, sit back and await release from the "horn", suffering little in consequence. On occasion the necessity to pre-
serve law and order arose only because the King or Campbell
of Lochow, later of Argyll (or both in collaboration) encouraged disorders and rebellions so as to have the excuse of
taking drastic and concerted action. A good example of this
is found in the acquisition of Islay by Campbell of Cawdor in
1615 at the expense of Clan Donald.

Mention of Cawdor brings to mind one of the strategic
marriages referred to above. When the 7th Thane of Cawdor
died in 1494 he left only a daughter. Her mother was a Rose
of Kilravock and the Laird of Kilravock naturally destined the
heiress to marry one of his grandsons. Unfortunately for him
he was in trouble with the King at the time, and Argyll who
was Justice-General found it very simple to arrange that the
marriage should be entrusted to him, so of course he decided
she should marry one of his own kinsmen. He believed in
planning well ahead, for the lass was very young at the time.
To make sure his plan succeeded he sent his relative, Campbell of Inverliver, with sixty men to escort the little girl to
Inveraray, ostensibly to see to her schooling. Surely an im-

posing company to take one small lass to school. The Roses, her uncles, did not like it and pursued Inverliver whose sons (said to be seven in number) covering his retreat were wiped out. One of his party suggested that it was a sore price to pay as in any case the girl was weakly and might easily die on their hands before they got home. The answer shows how determined were Argyll and his kinsman that Cawdor should become theirs. Inverliver remarked dryly "She'll not die so long as there is a red-haired lass on Lochaweside!" Thus was the Campbell House of Cawdor founded. Muriel, the heiress, duly married Sir John, third son of Argyll, in 1510 and resigned her estates into the hands of her grandson, John, 3rd of Cawdor.

From 1600 onwards MacIain of Glencoe, and many others, must have looked on the developments going on in Argyllshire with apprehension. Mac Chailein Mhòir was very busy indeed, and his kinsfolk with him. MacIain of Ardnamurchan had gone and his lands were in Argyll's hands, so too with others; and now the ancestral home of Clan Donald, the large island of Islay, was threatened. Cawdor was the aspirant to those rich lands with Kintyre for good measure. The last Macdonalds of Islay, descendants of Ian Mòr, son of John, First Lord of the Isles, were in great difficulty. Cawdor, with Argyll to help him, had his eye on Islay. The time was ripe. Clan Donald of Islay adhered to the old religion. The Covenant was very powerful, and Campbell, seeing the drift, had joined the winning side. The sensitive conscience of Cawdor, like one of his ancestors ninety years earlier, was troubling him about the "barbarous" conditions prevailing in the Isles; and he was planning to bring "peace" to those distressful regions. Peace to him meant, of course, occupation by himself. His ancestor, who had been embroiled in various clan raids on the Macleans and had even murdered their Chief, Lachlan, had also been righteously indignant and had made proposals to the Crown asking for powers to pacify the turbulent islesmen! The King had seen through his scheme and that attempt failed. So the Cawdor of 1615 made another effort, and this time succeeded.

In spite of every effort on the part of Angus, Chief of Dunyveg, and his son, Sir James, to make their peace with the

King, Islay and Kintyre fell to the Campbells. The last stand at Dunyveg made by Angus Òg, brother of Sir James, ended that story. Angus was arrested and executed. His wife, Catherine, daughter of Duncan Campbell of Danna, and her two small boys were hailed before the Privy Council for rebellion. Their Campbell blood did not save them; but they wisely did not appear, knowing what would happen. What became of them no one knows. Sir James, the last Macdonald Chief of Islay, died in 1626 without issue. He had married Cawdor's sister; but that did not inspire any sympathy in Cawdor's breast. She gave Sir James no heir; so that difficulty, with the disappearance of Angus (who had also married a Campbell as we have seen!), his widow and sons, left the succession wide open. Cawdor and Argyll were not slow to react.

In opposition to these acquisitive methods of the Campbells, Clan Donald caused the King much trouble for totally different reasons. They were not on the make. They only wished to secure possession of what they had owned for generations. The King and his nominees were continually trying to acquire the lands of the ancient Lordship, now divided among the descendants of Somerled. In this way, not only Clan Donald suffered. Any Clan which had been part of the Lordship of the Isles, Macleans, Camerons and others felt the strain. Most of them suffered at the hands of the Crown and the Campbells.

From 1642, at the outbreak of the Civil War, until the Restoration in 1660 the Cavaliers and Roundheads of England were represented in Scotland by the Royal party and the Covenanter respectively. The Government of Scotland was doubly "Covenanting", for the National Covenant of 1638 was now reinforced by that rather shameful documents The Solemn League and Covenant" of 1643 by which, among other things, the Scots handed over Charles I to the Roundheads and by a strange coincidence received at the same time a handsome monetary subsidy for the maintenance of their armies. It must be pointed out that the Scots who did this were not the Highlanders, unless one cares to include the Clan Campbell, whose Chief had become a staunch Covenanter, while his clansmen probably "cared for none of these

things" like Gallio of old. Montrose, who had signed the
National Covenant but later disagreed with the intransigent
methods of the other signatories, was the most successful
Royalist leader; while Argyll and Leslie were the leading
men on the other side, backed up in a rather uneasy alliance
by the armies of the Parliament. Many Scots were torn between these two factions—on the one hand their innate respect
for their Kings, and on the other their consciences in religious
matters. Montrose was a good example of this struggle going
on within individuals; and there must have been others like
him. Many efforts were made to reconcile the two issues; but
the actions of Charles rather hampered his supporters than
helped them. The clans who adhered to the old religion had
no such difficulties. They just supported the King as their
natural duty; and any inconsistencies or vacillations of which
he may have been guilty did not touch them closely.

The War of Montrose was, for Clan Donald, the only
bright spot in this century. For one brief year they were able
to hit back and harry their enemies; and naturally they took
full advantage. By 1647, however, the star of Clan Donald in
Argyllshire had set. Alasdair Cholla Chiotaich, Montrose's
able lieutenant, was away in Ireland and dead. The remnants at
Dunaverty were murdered in a brutal and treacherous manner by the Army of the Covenant under Leslie, with the
Campbells and a Covenanting minister in attendance. The
Lamonts had been equally treacherously murdered by the
Campbells. These two massacres were much more thorough
and successful than the later Massacre of Glencoe, and yet
are not remembered so widely. It is true neither involved
the murder of folk who had given hospitality for weeks to
their murderers; but in both cases prisoners, who had been
disarmed under promises of fair treatment, were butchered
until even some of the butchers were sick. Unfortunately
religion was a prime factor in these crimes as indeed it entered
into the events of 1692. There must have been many watching
these events and wondering who would be next. Certainly
MacIain in Glencoe must have had his thoughts, isolated in
his lonely glen, far from kinsfolk and friends, with Breadalbane so near to the south.

At the time of Montrose's War the Chief of Clan Campbell

was Archibald, 8th Earl and 1st Marquis of Argyll, best known to Highlanders as Gilleasbuig Gruamach (Grim Archie). He had a very difficult life; but, while others were changing sides during the reign of Charles I, the Civil War, and the Restoration, he was a steadfast supporter of the Covenanters and the Presbyterian Kirk, and in the end suffered for his convictions.

After the campaign of Aberdeen and Fyvie Montrose was faced with the problem of how to pass the winter in comparative safety. He had about 3,000 men—mainly Highlanders. Alasdair Cholla Chiotaich was there with the Clan Donald of Ulster, Skye, ClanRanald, Glengarry, Keppoch and Glencoe. With them were Stewarts, Macleans and Camerons, men from Athol and Badenoch, all in agreement in their hatred of the Clan Campbell. So where better to winter than in the heart of Argyll's country? "It is a far cry to Loch Awe!" was a favourite saying among the Campbells, and Argyll probably thought himself safe. A Glencoe man offered to guide the army into Argyll's country and promised them fat cattle and good provender for their winter sustenance. This was Angus Mac Ailein Duibh, brother of Ranald of Laroch, of whom later. He kept his word. Montrose knew well how to make full use of the mobility of his lean warriors, as his previous campaigns had shown. They could march for miles over the roughest country unhampered by baggage and still find energy to attack an astonished enemy with all the fire of the traditional Highland charge with broadsword, targe and dirk.

Starting in early December 1644 Montrose's men marched from Athol up Glen Dochart and down Glenorchy to the banks of Loch Awe. Argyll heard of their approach and probably thought it a local raid, but not imagining for one moment that the whole force was heading for Inveraray. Indeed, surprisingly enough he went himself to Inveraray; but was not there for long before the shocking news came that Montrose and Alasdair were coming down Glen Shira. At once he embarked in a fishing boat and made his escape to his castle of Roseneath on the Gareloch, a convenient place from which to take off for Glasgow or Edinburgh should occasion demand.

For some pleasant weeks the clans regaled themselves with Campbell provender. During this invasion no one has been able to accuse Montrose or his men of atrocities committed on women or children. It is true that any male who offered resistance was killed, houses burned and cattle driven. Clanranald lifted 1000 head in a raid on Knapdale to forage for the army. Fortunately for the Campbells, and indeed for the Royal Army too, the winter of 1644/45 was mild; and neither side suffered nearly so much as they might have. However, the time came when the clans must retire. They knew the influence Argyll had with the Government, and guessed rightly that he would gather large forces, Government as well as his own, to follow up and try to retrieve the situation. So in mid-January, laden with their booty, the Royal Army marched out of Inveraray, past Loch Awe again and north through the Pass of Brander, crossing Loch Etive in boats provided by Campbell of Ardchattan, who was probably only too glad to see them go. Now they were in friendly country—Appin and Glencoe. The Glencoe men were able to visit their homes and leave with their grateful wives much spoil from their foes.

This business of disposing of the spoil was always a problem for any leader of a Highland army. War was made to pay in those days unlike now. Victory was almost worse than defeat for the general officer commanding. The loot must be taken home; and the Highlander did not see any point in winning a battle if he could not secure his gains. Montrose was the most successful general in holding the clans together; but even he could not overcome this propensity; and by the time he arrived at the south end of the Great Glen at Inverlochy he had a force of only 1,500 men, about half the number that had entered Inveraray. Argyll was hard on his heels; and at the other end of the Glen, near Inverness, Seaforth awaited him with 5,000 men of doubtful value, but still three times his numbers.

At Fort Augustus (Cille Chuimein) he saw he would have to meet one or the other and he chose to oppose the stronger first—Argyll. To march back down the Glen which was full of Argyll's spies and scouts, would be to advise him of his intentions. To wait would be fatal, for he would be taken front and rear by much superior forces. He seemed to be trapped. At this point Ian Lom, the Keppoch bard, came to the rescue. He offered to guide the army back to Inverlochy by a circuitous route known to few and surprise Argyll. The march that followed is one that surpasses many celebrated forced marches in history. The route, up Glen Tarff over the mountains to the head of Glen Roy, down Glen Spean and round the shoulder of Ben Nevis to Inverlochy, led them over the roughest country imaginable. Snow lay on the heights, and the tracks were only faintly discernible. The men had little food and no shelter, not that shelter was needed for they had no time to halt. Montrose's own son died a month later as a result of this desperate march. At dawn on 2nd February 1645 Argyll was suddenly confronted with an enemy who ought to have been miles away to the East. Campbell of Achnabreac, an experienced soldier, took command while Argyll betook himself to his galley to watch the battle; and, when all was lost and the slaughter of his clansmen was taking place, he sailed for home.

The tide turned, however. After the disaster of Carbisdale in 1650 Montrose was betrayed by Neil Macleod of Assynt for a load of meal from Leith, two-thirds of which were said to have been sour! He was executed and his head placed on a spike on the Tolbooth of Edinburgh.

Alasdair, after a brief campaign in Kintyre against superior forces, was driven out to Ireland, leaving his rearguard in Dunaverty at the southernmost tip of that peninsula, hoping to bring them succour from Antrim. That help never came, however, and the garrison was wiped out. Young Ranald of Sanda, who was still a babe in arms, alone survived through the bravery and resource of his nurse who smuggled him out wrapped in a Campbell plaid with a ring still preserved in the family of Sanda. The babe's father and grandfather both perished in the slaughter. Meantime Alasdair had met his end at Cnocanos in County Cork fighting against the Roundhead Army which was commanded by Muradach O'Brian, the Irish quisling. There he attacked with his usual fire, over-reached himself, was captured severely wounded, and murdered. Of the leading actors in this drama only Argyll survived, for a time. Eleven years later he too was executed and his head adorned the same spike on the Tolbooth of Edinburgh which had so recently borne the head of the Great Marquis.

Argyll died with great courage and composure, thus in some way redeeming his lost reputation; for on at least two occasions he had left his clansmen to their fate in a very cowardly manner—at Inveraray and Inverlochy. Once more, after the battle of Alford, he is reported to have fled in great haste, having provided, even before the battle commenced, relays of horses to bear him in safety from the field. The fiery Chief of Glengarry nearly caught up with him; but Argyll's foresight and careful planning saved him.

Gilleasbuig Gruamach was of course heartily hated by the Western Clans. Even his friends in the Government were not a little jealous of his power and disliked him. One story told about him shows that he was not always unmindful of the code of honour of the Gael. From the earliest times bards were respected. They said what they thought about dignitaries, and moved freely between opposing forces much as ambassadors or heralds do with impunity. Ian Lom, already referred to, the Keppoch bard, had always been very scathing in his dealings with the Campbells. Some of his satires are scurrilous and biting; and he made himself so obnoxious to that clan that Argyll offered a handsome reward for him dead or alive. John, like Argyll himself, has been acucused of cowardice at times, but this time he rose to the occasion and went personally to Inveraray to claim the reward. Argyll received him hospitably and with honour. While showing him round the Castle they came into a room hung with the heads of many fine trophies of the chase. The host asked John if he had ever seen such a fine collection of heads anywhere. "Yes," said John. "I have." "Where?" asked Grim Archie. "At Inverlochy!" Argyll allowed John to go free after all.

It is easy to see from the foregoing account, which covers only a fraction of the history of this time that the hatred between Clan Donald and Campbell must have been increased a hundred fold. During this period the Glencoe men appear twice only for special mention. During these campaigns they took their full share of the battles, hardships and gains. The first occasion was when Angus Mac Ailein Duibh guided the

Royal Army into the Campbell fastnesses: the second was when one of them figured in a strange duel.

Ranald, son of Alan Dubh of Laroch, was one of the most notable of the warriors of Clann Iain; and he enhanced his reputation by the exploit of the duel referred to. After one of the engagements of 1645 an officer of dragoons was taken prisoner, and was heard to make some highly derogatory remarks about the Highlanders' way of fighting with sword, targe and dirk. Their custom was to fire their pieces at the enemy, throw them away together with their plaids, and charge with sword in the right hand and dirk in the left, while the targe on the left arm provided extra cover. The dragoon went on to challenge any of them to a duel—his sword against their sword and targe. This was truly a bold challenge and rash too. Ranald took him up at once and offered to take him on with dirk and targe alone, the dragoon to go free if he won. The Englishman was at first a little doubtful if Ranald would keep his word; but Ranald told him all his clan would desert the army, as a matter of honour, if the bargain was not kept. So the duel went on, although a kinsman of Ranald's, Alan of Dalness, himself an accomplished swordsman, tried to dissuade him saying, "The sword alone is better than dirk and targe; and there is no knowing what will become of you!" Ranald replied, "I don't know what will happen to me; but the very devil is going to happen to him." Ranald won and the dragoon remained a prisoner; and Ranald was known thereafter as "Raonall na sgeithe" (Ranald of the Targe). He survived the wars only to fall a victim of the Massacre, by then an old man. His son too fell; but his grandsons, who were away from home, lived on, one of them becoming a bard famous locally for his humorous poems.

So at last the Restoration came, and things were happier for the loyal clans. But not for the Covenanters. Argyll lost his head. The Highland Host was billeted on the Covenanters of Ayrshire and Galloway. Among them were the Glencoe men who bore (it is recorded) in accordance with old custom, a bunch of heather, the Clan emblem, on a pole. We hear little of them after this, and assume they lived at peace, for as usual the Government took little notice of them so long as they remained quietly at home.

Just before the Revolution of December 1688 the Central Highlands were in a very unsettled state. Mackintosh was at feud with Lochiel and the Keppoch Macdonalds. Coll of Keppoch (known affectionately as Coll of the Cows from his skill in cattle-lifting) was now Chief of Keppoch. He did not like Mackintosh, for good reasons. When his father died young Coll was at the University of St. Andrews; but he had to desert his books to take up his task as Clan Chief. On his way home he was arrested in Inverness by Mackintosh and thrown into gaol in an effort to collect rents. Coll appealed to the Privy Council and was set at liberty; but he never forgot the insult. For years Mackintosh had been trying to collect the rents of Keppoch and Locheil for lands which he held originally from the Lord of the Isles but now under charter from the Crown; but which he had never been able to enjoy because Locheil and Keppoch just sat and refused to leave, carrying on their occupation of lands which had belonged to their clans for generations. It was just another case of the tenure of the old Lordship of the Isles being threatened by nominees of the King of Scots under his feudal system of land-tenure. The Highlanders, least of all those who inherited from the old Lords of the Isles, never understood nor did they like the feudal allocation of lands to overlords, whom they regarded as little better than foreigners.

Mackintosh now made a desperate effort to assert his rights, and raising his clan and enlisting aid from the Government he advanced into Lochaber in force. Coll was not ready for such action and retired to the hills until he could collect his men. Mackintosh occupied Keppoch House and awaited results. They came. Coll looked for Mackintosh, and Mackintosh's forces, under Captain Donald Mackenzie of Suddie, looked for Coll. Both succeeded in their quest and the battle was joined at Mulroy in Glen Spean where this, the last clan battle, was fought. Coll had the advantage of the hill (Cothrom a' Bhràigh), a position always sought by Highland armies whence they could bring off one of their famous charges which usually decided the matter in a few minutes. Clan Chattan were routed and Captain Mackenzie slain, contrary to Coll's orders who did not wish to implicate the Government. The aged Chief of Mackintosh was made an

honoured prisoner at Keppoch House until the arrival of the
Macphersons in force, late for the battle, but in time to aid
their Chief, forced Coll to release him. But the Keppoch
lands remained in Coll's hands and he paid no rents until the
end of the century.

Coll remained under arms from this time until the Revolution and filled in his time very profitably by raids on Clan
Chattan lands. He even occupied the town of Inverness for a
time, and levied a toll of 4,000 merks. This was not forthcom-
ing for some time; and Coll waited with his force of some
1,000 men, which consisted of more than his own clan. The
Glencoe men were with him, and some of the Clan Cameron
who found the enterprise congenial, although they were there
without the open consent of their chief. This was the position
when Dundee flouted the Convention and came north to
raise an army for King James. Coll's contingent was the
nucleus of that army, ready for the rising of 1689.

Chapter Four

REVOLUTION 1688 AND WAR 1689-90

In June 1688 William of Orange, Stadtholder of the Neder-
lands, was invited in writing to cross the Channel and "secure
the liberties of the English (and presumably also the Scottish)
people". His claim genealogically was not very strong, but
his wife was the eldest daughter of James II, so when it came
to the time to mount the throne his wife was the senior
partner of a sort of dual monarchy, if a monarchy can be dual.
He was not at first offered the throne; but must have known
that that must follow. The names of the signatories to this
document show how seriously James had offended so many
important persons of such diverse character and interests.
From that time William planned his "invasion". Meantime
James swithered and did little beyond calling in his regular
troops from Scotland. William landed at Torbay on the 5th
November 1688 and advanced slowly on London. With him,
on the same ship, came Sir James Dalrymple, later Viscount
Stair.

Sir James had been Lord President of the Court of Session,
but had lost that post and retired to Holland as he felt James
did not trust him, and anything might happen. Even when he
was pardoned he preferred to stay in Holland, rather than
risk a recurrence of the King's displeasure. His life had not
been very happy, although successful in many ways. His wife,
Margaret Ross of Balniel, was a very managing woman of
strong and determined character. So successful was she in the
management of her husband's estates and the marriages of
her daughters that local opinion credited her with being a
witch. Of course at that time if anyone was rather more than
ordinarily prosperous or successful the machinations of the
Devil were suspected. One of her daughters is the original

"Bride of Lammermoor", as that story was founded on the
strange rumours that went round when Janet Dalrymple was
married to Dunbar of Baldoon. It was said she had murdered
her husband on the wedding night. This is quite untrue as
Baldoon died in 1682 by a fall from his horse. The bride
was not so lucky for the entries in the register are short and
not very informative. "Married August 12: led home
August 24: died September 12: buried September 30 1669."
The cause of death is not stated. With that brief account we
have to be content, and hope that the lady's short life was not
too unhappy. Lady Stair, wife of Sir James, died in 1692.

While Sir James was landing with William at Torbay, his
son Sir John, Master of Stair was in Edinburgh. He it was
whose name was later irrevocably linked with the Massacre.
He was born in 1648 and married in 1669 to Elizabeth,
heiress of Sir James Dundas of Newliston in West Lothian.
His fortunes changed with great rapidity; but, after being in
the common gaol for a space, he was set free in January 1686.
In December of the same year he went to London, and by
February of 1687 came back with the new position of King's
Advocate. In this office he had at times to institute proceedings against the Covenanters of the South-West—the ones
who at an earlier date he and his father had sheltered and
been prosecuted in consequence. However, changes did not
seem to trouble him. While in this position he sometimes had
to express sorrow at his father's attitude to the régime which
employed him, while Sir James in Holland deplored the
behaviour of his son. However, these differences were soon
to be resolved. Stair was Lord Justice-Clerk when William
landed and he quickly changed sides. Later he was one of the
Commissioners sent to London to offer the Crown of Scotland to the new King. He now became the main link between
the Convention in Edinburgh and the King in London. He
was appointed Lord Advocate in 1690 and one of the principal Secretaries of State from 1691 till 1695, when the
inquiry into the Massacre obliged him to resign. This was no
permanent set-back, however, as he was created Earl of
Stair in 1703. With the other guilty men his reward was
promotion.

The regular troops recalled from Scotland by James to

assist in the defence of the realm against William's "invasion", were a troop of Life Guards, Claverhouse's Horse (The King's Own), Dunmore's Scots Greys (Tam Dalyell's old regiment, which he had raised for Charles II at his estate of the Binns), Douglas's Foot Guards, and Buchan's Regiment (later the 21st Scots Fusiliers), in all about 3000 men. Claverhouse commanded the cavalry.

John Graham of Claverhouse was notable at this time as one of the few who stood by his King in adversity, till the end of his reign, and after. He was born in 1648, educated at St. Andrews University and became a Lieutenant in Lockhart's Regiment with the Scots' Brigade in Holland under William of Orange, at a time when Hugh Mackay of Scourie was Captain in Dumbarton's Regiment (The Royal Scots, 1st of Foot). There he met his future opponent for the first time. In 1677, having done William a service during a retreat by finding him a horse at an awkward moment, he was promised promotion; but, when the post fell vacant, it was given to another, some say to Mackay. In 1678 he left the Brigade and returned to Scotland, where he was given a commission to keep order in the Dumfries and Annandale area. His dealings there are too well known to need repetition here. Enough to say that he made his name detested among the supporters of the Covenant. He was a Royalist first and foremost and the King's enemies were his. The West country Covenanters certainly were no friends of the King; and, while there were many godly men who suffered martyrdom at the hands of the Royal troops, there were also others if the Master of Stair, himself at one time on the side of the Covenant, is to be believed. He once wrote that their conventicles "attracted the idle, debauching curious and harbouring criminals". Perhaps this was written after the time when he seemed, for a time at least, to attach himself to the Royal party. In any case we are now dealing with Claverhouse as touching the "Glorious Revolution", and can only say that his behaviour towards his royal master and the régime in which he sincerely believed was intensely loyal and steadfast.

Acting with Claverhouse in his support of King James was Colin Lindsay, Earl of Balcarres; and these two were, in the

event, the last friends to whom James was able to talk before
his final departure. Both suffered for their single-mindedness
in different ways. At the end James felt very much alone.
Even his family had deserted him: the troops he had led to
Salisbury to face William's expeditionary force were unreliable: the officers went over to the enemy one by one: and
James had perforce to fall back on London. There Claverhouse and Balcarres tried to induce him to make a stand; but
in vain. The two friends asked him to write a placatory letter
to the Convention in Edinburgh and retain the support at
least of the Scots. Then, when James had gone and William
had arrived, they met the latter, who tried hard to win them
over to his side. Both remained unmoved and left for the
North, Claverhouse at the head of his faithful few troopers.
Some forty of his own regiment would not part from their
commander.

Claverhouse was now a Viscount, having been created
Viscount Dundee by James not long before the crisis. From
being the "Bluidy Claverse" of the Covenanters he had
become the "Bonnie Dundee" of history, although it is
doubtful if that name was given him before Sir Walter Scott
wrote his famous ballad of that name.

Dundee, who was now forty years old, had married the
most unexpected bride, Lady Jean Cochrane, youngest
daughter of the Earl of Dundonald, a staunch Covenanter.
Lady Dundee had an exciting life, and can scarcely have
suffered from boredom. She came of a spirited family, however, and no doubt went through it all bravely. A lady of her
family had gone so far as to dress up as a highwayman and
hold up a messenger from the King with a warrant for the
execution of her father. The delay before another warrant
could be obtained was long enough for a change of policy and
her father's life was saved. Lady Dundee would have done a
like deed if it would have helped her husband; but, although
her life was full of action, we do not hear a great deal about
her. Her honeymoon was interrupted by her husband being
called away to disperse a conventicle which did not exist, or
at any rate was not there to be dispersed when he arrived on
the scene. Then, just when she was expecting the arrival of
their first-born child, a foreign king had to land and embroil

her husband in political strife. When the child was born, a
son, she was at home at Dunhope, and Dundee was at home
too, for once. The birth of a son made them both happy; but
it was attended by many upsets, alarms and excursions. The
birth was on the 9th April, ten days after the father had been
proclaimed rebel. William and Mary were proclaimed on the
11th, and on the 16th Dundee left home for the last time. It
is possible the couple met for a short time during Dundee's
swift raid down from Lochaber to Perth; but we do not know
for certain. A few years after Dundee's death, she married
Lt.-Col. William Livingstone, an old comrade in arms of
Claverhouse; but both she and her child by that marriage
were killed by the accidental collapse of the roof of an inn in
Utrecht in 1695. Hers was an exciting life, full of the rattle
of sabres and clatter of horses' hooves. Poor lady, she must
have needed all the courage of her race to put up with it
all.

In circumstances like these, Dundee, with a young wife and
newly-born son living on a nice little estate, might have been
forgiven if he had hedged, swithered or even changed sides;
but he kept hoping the royal cause of his King would triumph
in the end; for he expected some action from James along the
lines he and Balcarres had suggested at their last meeting. If
James would only try to conciliate his enemies, even those in
Scotland alone, anything might happen. Or so he saw it.

A Convention was set up in Edinburgh on the 14th March
1689. Stair was there, member for the burgh of Stranraer.
Dundee and Balcarres waited for the expected letter to arrive
from James. It came; and was nothing like they had anticipated. Someone had intervened in London. Clearly William
would soon be proclaimed King of Scots; and their lives were
now in danger. Dundee galloped out of the city on the 18th
March by the Leith Wynd and directed his route, still
attended by his faithful few, along the ridge where the new
town now stands. He paused only long enough to scale the
Castle rock and hold a parley with the Duke of Gordon who
held out for James. Dundee tried to confirm Gordon in his
stand, and left for home, where he quietly awaited the birth
of his first-born. Balcarres retired more unobtrusively to his
home in Fife. Dundee had been at home a bare week when

on the 28th March a summons came from the Convention
requiring him to lay down his arms and submit to the new
order. He replied that he was not under arms, was at home
attending to his family affairs and did not intend to appear
before the Convention. He knew Edinburgh was not safe
for him any more. The Convention at once proclaimed him
"rebel and fugitive" at the cross of Dundee. Balcarres was
arrested and put in the gaol at Kirkcaldy and later removed to
Edinburgh Castle.

For Dundee there were only two courses open now: to flee
to France as some were doing, or to take to the hills and try
to emulate the exploits of another Graham who had fought
for the Stuart cause, the great Montrose. He chose the latter
—to go North where he could find a ready-made army of
loyal supporters for the royal cause. As one of his enemies
said, he was nothing if not consistent. He left home on the
16th April. With him went his loyal troop of horsemen.

His movements from that day until the end were rapid and
bold. Like Montrose he seemed to have wings, turning up
in the most unexpected places at the most unpredictable times.
Once he even tried to get home to meet the very dragoons
who had been sent to arrest him, because he knew they would
desert to his side if he could only talk to them face to face.
Unfortunately the pedestrian Mackay, now a Major-General,
was plodding north; and he got in the way, quite inadver-
tently! So Dundee had to return to the hills; and to elude
Mackay he left the easy roads in the valleys and put three
mountain ranges between himself and his pursuers.

Hugh Mackay of Scourie was himself a Highlander but
seemed to have very little knowledge of the mobility of a
Highland army, or indeed Highland temperament at all. The
fact that Mackay got the promotion which had been promised
him by William was probably the reason for Claverhouse
leaving the Scots Brigade in 1678 and coming home so
hurriedly. No doubt the Covenanters devoutly wished he
had stayed in Holland. The two met again in July 1689 and
both lost a battle.

Dundee arrived in the north just in time to save the town of
Inverness from the unwelcome attentions of the enterprising
Coll of Keppoch with his mixed force of Macdonalds of his

Memorial Cairn erected in 1883 by Mrs. Ellen Burns-Macdonald, last
representative of the MacIains of Glencoe (the wreath is one laid
annually by the Clan Donald Societies all over the world) (*photo:*
Scottish Tourist Board).

Looking into Glencoe from the north side of Loch Leven at Callart
(*photo:* John Leng, Dundee).

View from A'Chioch (The Pap) of the lower Glen, the shore road to
Ballachulish, Eilean Munde (in foreground, wooded), Ferry, Loch
Linnhe and the Ardgour hills (*photo:* J. B. White, Dundee).

own clan and those of Glencoe with some Camerons who had
joined him in the adventure although their Chief was not out
with them on this occasion. Dundee managed to persuade Coll
to raise the siege and promised himself personally to find the
ransom money. It must be remembered that the town of
Inverness was inhabited mainly by any but Gaelic speaking
Highlanders. It was a market town on the edge of the Highlands, and the burghers were Lowland merchants and even
some foreigners. Coll, somewhat unwillingly, retired to the
west with the loot; and Dundee found, like others before him,
that he could do nothing with a force of clansmen until the
loot was safely deposited at home, and they saw prospects of
the next adventure producing some more. This certainly
applied at this time to Coll's men; but on occasions the clans
showed that they could sacrifice everything for an ideal with
no hope of material gain coming out of it. No wonder that
the Lowlanders, and least of all a foreign King, could not
understand the clans and their chiefs.

While awaiting the return of the Highlanders Dundee
made a lightning raid on the town of Perth, levied money he
regarded as due to his King, found a much needed string of
remounts for his hard-riding troopers, and retired again
northward. On this journey he may have had time to see his
wife and son in Glen Ogilvy, but we are not sure. Thence he
went north-west to recruit his Highland army. In Lochaber
he found Coll again under arms with Glencoe, Locheil, Glengarry, and the men of the Isles, Sleat, ClanRanald, Maclean
and others. Meeting Locheil and Glengarry he found they
had each received letters from Mackay offering them in the
name of William handsome rewards for their defection from
the standard of James. Locheil handed his to Dundee un-
opened and asked him to draft a suitable reply; while Glengarry told him the letter had already been answered—tersely
and to the point! The training of the army now went on, on
the ground later to be used by our own commandos in
1940/45 whose memorial stands looking over that historic
plain between Loch Lochy and the sea at Inverlochy. In particular they were taught how to receive a cavalry charge.
Although they did not need that technique in the event,
the practice of holding their fire until it could do the

4

most execution was valuable on the field of Killiecrankie.

The story of Dundee's last battle, of which he had seen many, for he was known to the Highlanders as Iain Dubh nan Cath (Black John of the Battles), is quickly told, and very well known.

Blair Castle, the seat of the Duke of Athol, which commanded the main road to the North, had been taken by Patrick Steuart of Ballechin and held. Athol was conveniently away in Bath taking the waters, and being "pumped" at intervals by his lady wife. His son, Lord John Murray, acting for him, tried to take the castle but failed. Athol was pro-William or at least somewhat Laodicean in his attitude. Mackay, who by now (July 1689) had brought his army south from Inverness to Edinburgh, like another General later (Cope in 1745), set out for the north again to seek out the enemy. His march was directed along the easy road through Dunkeld and Blair, and of course he wanted to drive Steuart out of Blair Castle as a preliminary to opening the campaign in the North. He had little news of Dundee's whereabouts until the final battle opened on the evening of the 27th day. After struggling through the narrow pass, he deployed on the fields below Urrard house on a spot known to Highlanders as Raon Ruairidh, and that is the name given by them to the battle. So Rory's Field became the site of one of the quickest victories in military history, an honour shared by Prince Charles's army at Prestonpans almost sixty years later. As Mackay emerged into the open and drew up his troops he found that Dundee had occupied, no doubt on the recommendation of the chiefs who knew their men, the higher ground overlooking Rory's Field, and was awaiting him instead of attacking while he came through the pass. In a word the clans had *cothrom a' bhraigh*, that advantage of the brae which gave them a good start in their wild charge—an opening move which usually caused much heart-searching in the breasts of their enemies.

On the right of the Highland army were the Macleans under their Chief, Sir John, with about 500 men. Next came ClanRanald under the young Chief, Alan, aged sixteen, with his brother-in-law, Donald of Benbecula, as Tutor after the Highland custom of the nearest male relative of ability and experience undertaking the education and training of the Chief while yet a minor. He brought about 700 men to the field. Next came some 300 Glengarry men under Alasdair Dubh, son of the aged Chief, Ranald, who stayed at home. Alasdair was a grim warrior who fought with the greatest valour here and later at Sheriffmuir in 1715, where young Alan of ClanRanald fell in his prime, and was mourned deeply by the whole of Clan Donald. In the centre 600 Camerons fought under their own chief, Locheil, and the redoubtable Coll of Keppoch with the Glencoe men, under old Alasdair of Glencoe, tall and belligerent for all his years. About 100 seasoned warriors followed MacIain and his two sons. On the left wing young Donald of Sleat led his regiment to the number of 500 with his uncle, Donald of Castleton, as Tutor and adviser. Castleton was by this time a grandfather, having led out the Sleat men on behalf of his brother, Sir James Mòr, in Montrose's War.

By a strange fate, Locheil's second son was in Mackay's army, a young subaltern in the Scots Fusiliers. A fellow officer is said to have remarked to young Cameron, "Well, there's your father up there with his band of savages!" To which Cameron replied that his father and his savages might come a bit closer to the red soldiers than they would like, and they had better be ready for a bitter fight.

Dundee's training must have been very thorough for the clans stood their ground under a galling fire and advanced close to the enemy before firing their muskets. It was here that severe losses were sustained by all the clan regiments. The officers mostly the relatives of the chiefs suffered most. The ground was open and there was a good field of fire. Ian Lom, the Keppoch bard, puts it, in his address to Sir Donald of Sleat, "On Raon Ruairidh of the blows, where you sustained the battle, you lost your gentry and trained officers. On the hard dry earth where a hare could not even hide her ear, you received the volley of lead. Unwavering were the heroes, wounded in the strife. . . ." Alasdair Dubh fought like a lion; but lost his own brother, Donald, and his son, Donald Gorm, who killed eighteen of the foe before falling. Donald of Sleat lost five cousins facing Mackay's right flank which was the only part of his army to show any fight. Among

these were Ranald, son of Castleton, James of Aird and
James of Capstill, whose cows at home on that very evening
had given blood in their milk. By this his family guessed
he had fallen long before the news came verifying their fears.

When the clans charged a terrible vengeance was taken
for these losses. In five minutes Mackay's army was driven
pell-mell back through the "crooked woods" of the Pass with
the loss of 2000 of his troops. Killiecrankie is held to be
derived from the Gaelic "Coille Chnagaidh" which is a very
apt description of the timber thereabout. *Cnag* can also
mean a snap of the fingers or a blow; and certainly there
were many *cnagan* that day and that might well be the
origin of the name.

Mackay is credited with a force of about 4,500 troops, and
Dundee 2,500. The latter figure may be an underestimate as
Clan Donald alone must have had about 1,700 men in the
field. In any case it was a notable victory of a small number of
irregular warriors defeating a greater formation of regular
soldiers.

The victory lasted a few minutes only, for Dundee fell at
the head of his small band of horse in the heat of the battle;
and that at once turned it into a defeat. The cause was lost;
and untold suffering followed. If there had been no Killiecrankie there would have been no Massacre; and without
Glencoe to inflame the Jacobites there might have been no
further risings, always provided William and his advisers
and successors had tried to understand the clans and their
need for an outlet for their energies and spirit of enterprise.
It is useless to speculate. Everyone must form his own
opinion as to what might have happened had Dundee lived;
just as later there are so many theories as to what might have
happened if Princes Charles had succeeded in his rising of
1745/46. Enough to say that Killiecrankie led inevitably to
the tragedy of Glencoe less than three years later.

How Dundee fell is a subject upon which there is some
disagreement. Some say he raised his arm to wave his men
on thus exposing a joint in his corslet through which a bullet
passed into his breast. The bullet was said to have been of
silver according to those who believed only such a bullet
could have slain one who was in league with Satan! Others

again say he was shot through the head. He lived long enough to hear that the battle went well for King James, and died, murmuring his satisfaction at that news. Although the chiefs had begged him to direct the battle from the rear he refused indignantly, asking them what sort of a commander warriors like theirs would think him if he saved his skin while others died. At the moment of his death his friend, Balcarres, now a prisoner in Edinburgh Castle, woke and saw his old comrade standing looking steadfastly at him. Jumping up joyfully he rose to greet him, thinking he had come to set him free. But Dundee silently beckoned to him and disappeared, and Balcarres knew he was dead.

It did not take long for the Highland army to melt away after this. Generals Cannon and Buchan were distrusted by the Highlanders, and few remained to suffer the defeat of Cromdale in May 1690 which put an end to the rising. It is not likely that old Alasdair MacIain and his men were at Cromdale because we know what happened on their way home through Breadalbane's country; and that area was just the way they would go from Killiecrankie homewards. Flushed with victory they could not resist the temptation of making a *creach* on their homeward journey. Fat Campbell cattle lay in their path; and what more natural than to avail themselves of some of the opportunities offered? As it turned out they overdid it; for that *creach* was never forgotten. "Ne Obliviscaris" is the Campbell motto, and in this case they followed its advice faithfully. According to Campbell sources MacIain collected 240 cows, 36 horses, 993 sheep, 133 goats and many household goods. The value was assessed at £7,540 sterling! This was surely one of the most successful raids in Highland history, which abounds in examples, although in most of them we are left to make a guess at the monetary value of the takings. This loss quite beggared the family of Campbell of Glenlyon and the laird. Robert, who met MacIain later, was obliged to take up military service in Argyll's regiment to support himself and his family. This has to be recorded as some small extenuation of his behaviour later. In any case it fomented the already deep and long-standing hatred getween the two clans, which we have tried to trace in preceding chapters.

The rising having failed, the Government at once took steps to try to "pacify" the chiefs and their clans. Two frigates were sent to overawe Sir Donald of Sleat, who killed twenty men of the landing party and drove the rest back to their ships. Glengarry one day espied a company of soldiers approaching his castle along the south shore of Loch Oich in order to occupy it. An ancient retainer of his who had spent much time polishing the guns on the turrets begged to be allowed to use them as he had never had a chance of trying them out. Alasdair Dubh did not think much of such new-fangled weapons: for him the broadsword which he could wield so well; but to placate the old man he consented to having them fired. The first shot fell wide; but the second knocked the officer off his horse and the whole company retired to Inverness. It was some time, however, before the chiefs made their peace with the Scots Parliament, and King William. It took nearly two years, many schemes, some good and some bad, and a massacre to achieve an uneasy peace for the next twenty-three years.

One can imagine the rage that must have overcome Dutch William when he heard the news of Killiecrankie, for the first bulletins did not include a report of the death of Dundee. The Highlands were a distant and unknown land even to most of the Lowland Scots, inhabited by a foreign folk who spoke a strange tongue, and followed barbarous ways of life. Even as late as 1745 the inhabitants of England thought the High-landers were cannibals. William, a stranger, even in London, regarded Edinburgh as the back of beyond and the Scots as hardly civilized according to his lights. How much farther away in distance and culture must the clans have seemed to him! His main obsession was to oppose and defeat Louis XIV of France, and here was a band of remote savages daring to rise against his rule and threaten to upset his plans. He was only just getting along with the English in the first year of his reign. Many of the Scots, the place-seekers mainly, were falling into line; and these misguided tribes in the North were rebelling. To him it must have seemed very un-reasonable, and his wrath was fertile ground in which the schemers could sow their seed.

One biographer says that "William was swift to decide and

execute, calm in judgment, resolute in purpose, serene and immovable in the face of tumult and danger. But he was ready on occasion to sanction acts of ruthless cruelty, and he often showed considerable lack of scruple and some indifference to high principles. His cold and keen nature made him deficient in sympathy, and unable to consider or even to perceive other views than his own." Before coming to Britain he had already shown these traits in his cynical treatment of De Witt, when the revolution which overthrew him led to the brutal murder of his brother and himself by the mob. On that revolution William climbed to power and he seemed cold and callous on that occasion. The all-absorbing passion to restore the balance of power in Europe led him to sweep aside ruthlessly any who got in his way. Britain was to him a heaven-sent recruiting ground for forces to help him achieve his objective, and anyone who stood in the way must be pitilessly dealt with, especially an obscure tribe in a distant corner of his newly acquired realm.

After Cromdale in May 1690 the Jacobite chiefs kept in touch and seem to have been the only consistent element in the country. Everyone knew what they believed and where their loyalties lay. They made that abundantly clear. They refused submission until King James absolved them from their vows. Meantime the Government halted between at least two opinions—should the clans be rooted out, or would it be possible to bribe them into submission? The unfortunate soldiers, Mackay, Sir Thomas Livingstone who succeeded him, and Colonel Hill at Fort William, received impossible orders which were frequently countermanded before they could be carried out or even tried. On one occasion Hill was told to "fall upon" the clans in his neighbourhood. These orders worried him quite a lot as he had gained the confidence and even friendship of those around him, notably Locheil. To his intense relief the order was cancelled soon after. He knew he could not carry it out. His men were unreliable. Their morale was at a low ebb due to arrears of pay, and lack of supplies. Colonel Hill himself was very depressed. He had served the Government faithfully for years and even his pay was sadly overdue. He was expected to build up his fortress with very few supplies and unenthusiastic workmen. The

Commander in Chief, Livingstone, and his officers knew that any attempt to "root out" Locheil, Glengarry, Keppoch, Appin and Glencoe would take a very long time even if it could be done at all. One at a time, perhaps; but all at once— impossible. And they were all of one mind in their antagonism to William until they got leave from their rightful King to hand in their submission.

Faced with these hard facts the Government resorted to bribery; and this is where the name of Breadalbane, one of the chief actors in the tragedy, comes on the scene. It was his bright idea that the clans could be won over with money, not an unlikely supposition for a Campbell to make, although he ought to have known better.

The Campbells of Breadalbane descend from Black Colin of Glenurchy, second son of Sir Duncan Campbell of Lochow by his wife, the Lady Marjory Stewart. Hence the patronymic of the House of Breadalbane—Mac Chailein Mhic Dhonnachaidh (Son of Colin, son of Duncan). In 1432 Sir Colin received from his father the estate of Glenurchy from which the Macgregors had been driven.* The methods by which the Glenurchy family became Earls (and later Marquises) of Beeadalbane is shortly explained in the *Highland Papers*, Vol. LV, page 198, where we find under the heading "Glenurchy writs" the following: "The three writs that follow were supplied by J. M. Mayne Campbell Esq. and illustrate the foundation of the House of Glenurchy, now Earls of Breadalbane. The Lairds of Glenurchy coveted their lands and consistently pursued a policy of ruthless harrying of their less powerful neighbours till they got the whole country into their hands. The same policy brought Duncan Campbell of Glenurchy into the plot to murder the 7th Earl of Argyll and the notorious Ian Glas to devise the Massacre of Glencoe". Which is just another and neater way of describing the methods we have already noticed in previous chapters.

John Campbell, son of Sir John of Glenurchy and his wife the Lady Mary Graham, was born in 1635, backed King Charles in the Glencairn rising in 1653, and sat in Parliament from 1669 to 1674. He was a man of great ingenuity and

* Lord Lyon: *Clans and Families of Scotland*, page 92.

acumen, but was described by one of his contemporaries as "a man of fair complexion, with the gravity of a Spaniard, as cunning as a fox, wise as a serpent, but as slippery as an eel". In a very short space of time he was able to elevate himself from a baronetcy to an earldom. It happened like this. He had lent money to George Sinclair, Earl of Caithness, and when Sinclair died he foreclosed on the estate. The male relatives of the deceased very naturally claimed their rights. Glenurchy took steps. In 1678 he married the widow, and in 1680, as the Sinclairs were still adamant, invaded Caithness with a force of clansmen among whom was Robert Campbell of Glenlyon. He had seven hundred men with him. They were enough for his purpose. The Sinclairs under command of the Laird of Keiss met him on their own ground at a stream, not inappropriately called Allt nam Meirleach (The Stream of the Robbers), and were signally defeated. Glenurchy became Earl of Caithness, for a time. However, the Sinclairs invoked the aid of the powers in Edinburgh and one of them was made Earl of Caithness while Glenurchy was consoled by being made Earl of Breadalbane. This raid took him a long way from home and it is hard to understand how he did it unless one remembers that raiders paid for free passage through their neighbours' territory by giving them a percentage of the profits. None of the clans would worry much about an expedition into Lowland country; and Caithness is outside the Highland Line anyway. This is pointed out forcibly in the Campbell pibroch composed by Finlay MacIvor, Glenurchy's piper, at the battle. This tune is known as "Bodaich nam Briogais" (The Carles with the breeks) and was supposed to convey to the kilted Campbells that their enemies, who wore the trews, were on the run.

This ability of a pibroch to carry a message may seem strange and even impossible, but several instances occur where it is undoubtedly true, and many a pibroch has words traditionally linked with it. These may have been composed later, but at the time they seem to have been well understood by the hearers. Pipers of the old school will often aver that pipe-music, especially the classical music of the pipe, the pibroch, speaks in Gaelic. One famous example will suffice. When Colla Ciotach, father of the famous Sir Alasdair already referred to in dealing with the War of Montrose, was driven out of Islay, he left a garrison in the castle of Dunnyveg. While he was away in Antrim gathering reinforcements, Cawdor took the castle. Coll approached all unsuspecting. His piper, who was among the prisoners, saw a galley far off and knew it to be his master's. He mounted the walls and played a tune which he composed on the spot. As Coll rounded the point and was about to enter the bay he heard the tune and at once understood the message conveyed by it, turned his birlinn and sailed away to safety. The pibroch, known as the Pibroch of Dunnyveg, certainly does seem to give a note of warning even if one does not know the words—*'Cholla mo rùn, seachain an Dùn, Seachain an Dùn, Seachain an Dùn.* (Coll, my beloved, avoid the castle!) Whether the Campbell pibroch told the clansmen something or not, a rousing tune on the bagpipe at the height of a battle has frequently inspired Gaelic warriors to superhuman efforts, not only in the old days, but even down to our own time. Strange to say the same tune, composed at Allt nam Meirleach, comes up again in the course of this story, with words far different from those used at the Robbers' Stream.

John Campbell, created Earl of Breadalbane in 1681 and Privy Councillor in 1685, was now one of the most powerful members of the Scottish Government. When Dundee seemed to be prospering he communicated with the Jacobite leader in a very tentative way; for Dundee writes that "Breadalbane keeps his house pretending the gout!" In fact Breadalbane was trying, not to sit on the fence which would be a painful exercise for one suffering from gout, but to keep a foot on each side. He succeeded in landing on the winning side. When the Government was at a loss to know how best to deal with the clans who persisted in their loyalty to their King, he suggested that he be entrusted with £20,000 to buy the Chiefs over to the side of the new King. He did not get the full amount, but a rather naïve Parliament handed over £12,000 for the purpose. How they ever expected a Campbell to win the confidence of men like Locheil, Glengarry and the rest, is beyond the comprehension of anyone who knew those gentlemen; but he received the money and called a meeting of the chiefs. This meeting took place at his own house on the Tulla Water at Achachallader looking out over his own hills of Glenorchy—his own now, but originally Macgregor country. Unfortunately the Clan Gregor had fallen foul of the Government many years before and the Campbells had stepped in on the old, old plea of "restoring law and order".

The chiefs duly met at Breadalbane's house on 30th June 1691; but the meeting did little except to benefit Breadalbane, as might have been forecast. Instead of money, threats and airy promises were handed out. Alasdair of Glencoe in particular was informed that any money due to come his way would be kept back as a contra-account for the cattle lifted by him on his way home from Killiecrankie. He was furious and dryly remarked that they were being offered a remission for killing red-coated soldiers at Killiecrankie, but the lifting of a few cows was apparently no subject for pardon; and in any case no money could estrange them from their rightful King. The meeting broke up with little accomplished except that the chiefs undertook not to engage in hostilities before October of the year. Certain other private articles were agreed to. As they were private, and in their very nature understandably so, there is no proof of their authenticity. These were (a) the agreement was to lapse if a rising took place for any reason: (b) that James II had to give his consent before the chiefs would consider submitting to William: (c) messengers were to be allowed free passage to get that consent from James: (d) if William's forces were withdrawn the clans would rise, and lastly, and the most extraordinary of all, that Breadalbane undertook in the event of a rising to join the clans with 1,000 men! No wonder these articles were secret. That Breadalbane was secretly a Jacobite, as many of the chiefs believed, seems plain enough in view of his action later in the rising of 1715. None of these undertakings seems to have been the symptom of a true supporter of the existing Government. Indeed, the whole business helped the other side, if it did anything at all. Firstly, it encouraged the chiefs to continue to consider a rising was possible and might have greater backing than the previous one; and secondly, by offering bribes, part of which were obviously going to be withheld, it antagonized some of the chiefs, whose discontentment reflected on the whole spirit of the meeting. When Colonel Hill reported the results of the meeting, with the content of the secret articles, everyone knew it would be impossible to prove them in court. Breadalbane wrote to Stair protesting innocence. Stair was on his side, and wrote "No body believes your lordship capable of doing either a thing so base, or that you could believe there could be any secret treaties, where there were so many ill eyes upon your proceedings; but the truth will always hold fast." Perhaps General Mackay was not far wrong when he described Breadalbane as "one of the chiefest fomentors of the troubles of the kingdom not for the love of King James, but to make himself necessary to the Government". The truth did hold fast—if not at this time at least in the later inquiry into the events preceding the Massacre.

The money, although unspent on the object in view, did not go back to the Treasury, so one has to be content with Breadalbane's own statement of account which would hardly satisfy the most haphazard business concern, let alone such a hard hearted body as the Treasury. When asked tactfully by the Earl of Nottingham about the manner in which the money had been disbursed, he replied in writing "My Lord, the Highlands are quiet, the money is spent, and that is the best way of accounting among friends." His injured innocence and irregular methods of book-keeping deceived no one. Nothing more was done about it.

The Master of Stair, although very much implicated with Breadalbane in this matter, was doubtful about the benefits of this transaction, for he writes in December 1691 to Breadalbane himself, "God knows whether the £12,000 sterling had been better employed to settle the Highlands or ravage them... I think Clan Donald must be rooted out, and Locheil. Leave the Macleans to Argyll." The last remark refers to Argyll's expedition to Mull. It was the old story. A clan gets into trouble with the Government and is at once fair game for Argyll to harass with Government sanction and support, of course. Mull was invaded, and Maclean escaped to his fortress of Carnaburgh in the isles to the west. Henceforth Argyll became feudal superior of that area. Troubled waters can be made to produce fish if one goes about it in the right way.

The money having been spent, and bribery having failed, there remained the other alternative—rooting out. Clan Donald was first on the list and the conspirators began their planning.

Chapter Five

PLANS FOR PEACE—THE THREE OATHS

WHILE the two alternatives of bribery and rooting out were being considered, another possible way of pacifying the clans was suggested by some, notably Mackenzie of Tarbat, later the Earl of Cromarty. This was that the superiorities should be purchased by the Crown and invested in the sovereign alone. For many years the feudal superiorities had irked the Celtic clans. Indeed the whole feudal system, which had first been applied to Scotland by Malcolm Canmore, his sons and their Norman friends, had always been in direct conflict with the ancient Gaelic ideas of clans headed by their patriarchical chiefs, who ruled by consent of the clan only. A chief who exceeded his powers could be removed and replaced by another member of his family more suited to the task, not so a feudal superior. In the ClanRanald, which most of all the clans cherished the old order of Gaelic tradition, two chiefs were deposed—one who made himself obnoxious by his cruelty was assassinated and his progeny for all time excluded from the succession: another was replaced by his uncle, who to the minds of the clansmen was much superior as a warrior and leader. When the deposed chief tried to reinstate himself with the help of his mother's kindred a bloody battle was fought, and the clan's wishes maintained. That was Blar na Leine in 1544.

The imposition of a feudal superior who was foreign in sympathies and outlook led to nothing but trouble. At one time Locheil, for example, held some of his lands from no less than three different superiors. One of these was Mackintosh whose claim dated back to the Lordship of the Isles, a claim which had lapsed with the forfeiture in 1492. Mackintosh, however, continued to press his claims not only to

Locheil's lands but the whole of Brae Lochaber held by Keppoch. It was irksome enough when Mackintosh held such a superiority; but when the Campbells acquired, in one way or another, superiority over the lands held by Maclean, MacIain of Glencoe, Ardnamurchan and others, the peace was well and truly disturbed, which led at once to the old "fire and sword" technique, a process which led to the acquisition of even more superiorities by Argyll and his kinsfolk.

A paragraph in the treaty agreement shows how important this matter of the removal of the superiorities was to the chiefs. They suggested "that King William should, at the public charges, free them from all manner of vassalage and dependence on the great men their neighbours, as King James was to have done, for which they produced his letters; that being thereby freed from tyranny and oppression of these superiors they might have their sole dependence on the Crown, and be enabled effectually to suppress thieving, and employ their people in the service of their country". This would seem to imply that the chiefs had begun to realize that some move to raise Highland regiments in the King's service might provide an outlet for the active members of their clans and such a scheme could be profitable to both sides. Some tentative moves had already been made in that direction in times past, but the time had not been ripe for such a radical change in the Highland way of life. Duncan Forbes of Culloden, Lord President between the risings of the '15 and '45, suggested the same scheme and was turned down by an apathetic government. Later it was adopted with success, and Pitt took the credit as though it were his own idea. How well those clansmen who enlisted in the Highland regiments fought and died is a matter of history. Some of them had even been soldiers in Prince Charles' army in '45. Here is one of those big "Ifs" of history. If Forbes' plan had been taken up after the '15, would there ever have been a '45?

The quotation in the above paragraph is from Locheil's *Memoirs* and shows that the chiefs realized better than their opponents how best to pacify the Highlands. However, such simple and straightforward steps were not acceptable to men like Stair and Breadalbane.

The King did not know much about such things, still less how important they were to his Gaelic subjects. Nevertheless, no doubt advised by someone who did know, in his orders to the Council in Scotland which accompanied the terms of the oath of indemnity required from the dissidents, he expressly included a promise that the superiorities would be purchased. In those orders he wrote, "We are resolved to be at some charge to purchase the lands and superiorities, which are the subject of these debates and animosities, at the full and just avail, whereby the Highlanders may have their imediat and entire dependence on the croune. And, since we are resolved to bestow the expense, must consider it as ill service done to us and the Countrey, if any concerned shall, through obstinacy or frowardness, obstruct a settlement so advantagious to our service and the public peace. And we doe expect from you the utmost application of our authority to render this design effectual; and that you will communicate our pleasure to the Governor of Innerlochie and other commandants that they be exact and diligent in their several posts; but that they show no more zeall against the Highlanders after their sub-mission than they have ever done formerly when they were in open rebellion." The last sentence is capable of some latitude of interpretation. When it came to the point of communicating the terms of the oath to the chiefs all reference to the King's desire to accede to their wishes in the purchase of the superiorities was omitted. By whom? Or at whose instigation? This omission removed the most attractive in-ducement to the chiefs to conform. It is obvious this must have been done at the command of some or all of the superiors affected, who of course had a powerful influence in the Council.

The whole position is summed up in the *Scottish Historical Review XVI*, p. 29 et seq., "The chiefs never had a really firm offer from the Government of the terms proposed as likely to lead to a real settlement. The necessary condition of success was that Argyll should surrender a power and position which his ancestors had long and painfully built up. . . . The superiorities were not bought, the money was not distributed." Argyll was obviously the one who would suffer most if the plan was carried out. He was in London,

Highland noble wearing Highland dress of the period, *c.* 1670. This portrait by John M. Wright (1625–1700) came from Taymouth Castle, the seat of the Breadalbane family. Though it is sometimes called "The Earl of Moray", it is also taken to be the first Earl of Breadalbane (which it may well be) painted after his successful raid on Caithness (*photo:* National Galleries of Scotland).

River Coe in Lower Glen, looking south to Bidean nam Bian, pictured from below Signal Rock, near Achnacon; An Sron on right (*photo: Scotsman* Publications).

River Coe, above the bridge, looking upstream (*photo:* John Leng, Dundee).

and a trusted adviser of the King's who consulted him frequently on all matters pertaining to the realm of Scotland This did not stop the King sending the orders mentioned above to the Council in Edinburgh; but there' they were deprived of the essential undertaking to remove the superiorities. Someone "through obstinacy or frowardness" did "obstruct a settlement so advantagious" and in so doing inflicted "an ill service to the King and the Countrey". It was not beyond the power of Argyll to let it go from London and stop the important part in Edinburgh.

Archibald, 10th Earl of Argyll, and later (1701) 1st Duke, was born in 1658. His mother was the Lady Mary Stewart, eldest daughter of the 4th Earl of Moray; and her wedding on the 13th May 1649 at Moray House in the Canongate of Edinburgh was the occasion for an unhappy incident, when the wedding party had the "entertainment" of watching the gallant Marquis of Montrose being led captive up the street to his place of imprisonment in the Tolbooth. As Lord Lorne, Archibald Campbell had opposed his father in the rebellion which led to the latter's execution on the 1st July 1685. Lorne offered his services to James II against his father; but was not required to implement that offer. When the 9th Earl died his estates were forfeited; but Balcarres prevailed upon James to settle a sum of £800 per annum on Argyll to be paid out of the forfeited estates. At the very time of the 9th Earl's execution Lorne's young son, John, later 2nd Duke, fell out of a third storey window, and took no harm, which was regarded as a good omen for the future of the family. Although the annuity had been settled, Argyll preferred to retire to Holland where he joined himself to the cause of William, and came over with him in 1688. From that time, now 10th Earl of Argyll, he was much in the company of the King. He it was who administered the coronation oath of Scotland to William, which was taken without demur except that William made special mention that he would countenance no sort of religious persecution or repression. A few days later the forfeiture was rescinded and Argyll came once more into his patrimony. In 1690 he became one of the Lords of the Treasury so must have known of, if indeed he did not have an active part in, Breadalbane's

financial enterprises. How far the confidence placed in him by
the King contributed to the Massacre of Glencoe it is very
hard to assess. Much could be done verbally with no record
left. It is true the *Encyclopaedia Britannica* (14th Edn.)
boldly states that the "refusal of the Macdonalds of Glencoe
to join in the submission to the King led Argyll to organize
the terrible massacre which has made his name notorious.
His political services were rewarded in 1701 by his being
created Duke of Argyll." The second sentence following so
closely on the first has a sinister ring about it. Certainly it
was his regiment that carried out the infamous orders; but
he was the Colonel and not the man to give the orders directly
to the soldiers, however much scheming may have gone on
in London.

Thus in August 1691 we find the actors in the tragedy
taking their places. Argyll in London, a trusted adviser of the
King: Stair, Principal Secretary of State for Scotland, and
virtual ruler of that realm, in constant touch with the King,
and, in his absence, the Queen: Breadalbane, the chosen
intermediary between the clans and the Government, a sort
of Minister without portfolio, trusted by Stair and no one
else: Sir Thomas Livingstone, Commander in Chief of the
forces in Scotland, with Colonel Hill under him as Governor
of the Fort of Inverlochy: and the clans under bond to cause
no trouble before October. All was quiet.

Back in May the Government had decided that the chiefs
must take an oath of allegiance to William. At the meeting at
Achachallader they made it quite plain that they would, if
James gave his consent; and an envoy was sent on their
behalf to James in France to get that consent. In fact, as has
already been stated, they were quite consistent in their
attitude, and everyone knew where they stood. The same can
hardly be said for the Government, civil or military. The
actions of the civil powers are to be traced later in the light
of letters and documents left on record. Meantime, what of
the forces under Livingstone's command?

The military establishment in October 1691 according to
the Army List is as follows:

Cavalry: A troop of Guards (in English pay); Sir Thomas
Livingstone's   own   Dragoons;   Colonel   Cunningham's

Dragoons; one other Dragoon Regiment. Each of these had 360 men, except for the Guards who numbered 450. Total: 1,500.

Infantry: The Regiments of Leslie, Leven, Lauder, Argyll, Buchan, and Hill: each stated to be 780 strong. Total: 5,000.

Of the above regiments two were implicated in the Massacre, Argyll's and Hill's. The history of Argyll's Regiment in the *Scottish Historical Review* says that "to show gratitude to the new Government and not without an eye to his own further interests, the new Earl proposed to raise a regiment of 600 men." It was accordingly raised in April 1689 with ten companies of sixty men in each. The Lt.-Colonel was Duncan Campbell of Auchinbreck, the Major was Robert Duncanson, and Robert Campbell of Glenlyon was among the Captains (Company Commanders). (For the personnel in the regiment in October 1691 see Appendix I.)

Hill's Regiment was raised by Colonel Hill in September 1690 and was made up of the remnants of Glencairn's and Kenmure's regiments, which had become uneconomic, as neither had enough men to keep up to strength. (For the roll of officers in Hill's Regt. in January 1692 see Appendix II.)

With an army like this Livingstone might have done something to put the clans out of action for good; but it would have taken a long time. In fact he at one time as good as asked permission fo root out all of them. Meantime this force had to be maintained and paid. The campaign of 1689 was said to have cost 150,000 sterling; and it was obviously the duty of the Scots Government, represented by Stair, to avoid another such, and yet cut down the expenses of prolonged diplomatic talks. However much he and Livingstone might have liked to root out the clans in a campaign of extermination, it would mean two or three years of costly operations on their own estimate. The expense and the loss of the services of 5,000 troops at a time when William's continental wars were so demanding could not be faced. Perhaps it was these problems and the impossibility of solving them by direct action that made the King, Stair and their minions decide to do it more economically by making a terrible example of the weakest member of the united front presented by the chiefs, thereby discouraging the rest.

Livingstone's task was not easy. In the summer of 1691 he had been ordered to concentrate his army in Badenoch in readiness to fall upon the clans. He was not at all happy about billeting a large force in the Highlands to eat up the supplies of the countryside and antagonize the inhabitants, unless he was to be allowed to attack them. To try to live peaceably among them would be too difficult. The orders were scarcely issued than they were countermanded. His troops too were not happy. In February Livingstone wrote "The troops of horse are in a very mutinous humour, having got no pay as troops, nor like to get any as dragoons. There are many of the troops who have taken their officers prisoners with the standards and trumpets, entered into a bond of association, and will not submit to any who would convince them to reason."

The Governor of Inverlochy Fort (later re-named Fort William), Colonel John Hill, was another rather bewildered commander. His service had been long and arduous. He began at Inverlochy as a Major under Monk, whose rule under the Commonwealth was much more acceptable to the clans than that of the Covenant, and was Governor there until 1698. Hill at this time made good friends of the local chiefs, notably Locheil. His dealings were honest and straightforward and the chiefs respected him. During the Commonwealth forts were maintained at Leith, Ayr, Perth, Inverness and Inverlochy. At the Restoration they were abandoned. When Inverlochy became once more a Government fort Hill came back and was again the spearhead of royal rule in that area. In May 1691 he reported that all was quiet. His troops patrolled the country round and were kindly received by the inhabitants. Hill's worries came much more from within than outside the Fort. He had served long and faithfully without much recognition of his services. His pay was in arrears. He was far from home. His duties were difficult, requiring a great knowledge of local conditions, and he was in fact irreplaceable. Stair thought so, for he expressed great concern when Hill fell ill, not knowing what he should do if Hill were to die. It would have taken any successor a long time to

settle down to handling the chiefs with diplomacy. In fact,
Hill was like so many of our race who have manned our frontiers among warlike tribes, getting to know and respect them,
laboriously finding out how to handle them and generally
acquiring that local knowledge which alone makes such tasks
possible. In addition he too suffered from the arrival of
impossible orders, only to have them countermanded (much
to his relief be it said) before they could be carried out. He
was short of officers too. He had a Major, John Forbes,
brother of the Laird of Culloden, whom he thought "a rash
young man". There was also a Captain; but Hill did not like
either very much; and they probably thought it no promotion
to be sent to a fort like Inverlochy. Hill's troops were not
happy either, being short of pay and amenities, living in a half-
built fort among clans who might rise at any time. Hill had
continually to complain about shortage of supplies and
materials and the unenthusiastic workmen repairing and
extending the Fort. Hill's regiment, being a recent amalga-
mation of two regiments, was raw and its morale could not
have been high.

On 29th August 1691 a royal proclamation was made
stating the terms of the Oath of Allegiance required from the
chiefs and their principal tenants. This superseded the oath
demanded after Cromdale in May. The earlier oath had not
been taken by the chiefs; but Hill reported that the "middle
men" were coming in in satisfactory numbers and he was
administering the oath to them. A notable case of this was
that of Achnacon and Achtriochtan, both of whom were
received by Hill, and his letter of indemnity was in their
pockets at the time of their death. So Hill seems to have had
the power to give the oath, and protection to those who took
it, up to August; but after the royal proclamation was made
the conditions altered, and a military commander had not the
power to give it. This transfer of that power from the
military authorities to the civil was the undoing of MacIain
and his gentry; the latter because they considered themselves
safe with Hill's letter in their possession, and the old chief
because he thought he had only to go to Hill at Inverlochy
and he would be accepted. The August proclamation expressly stated that those who had been in arms against the

King "should plead and take benefit of this our gracious indemnity, shall swear and sign the oath of allegiance to us by themselves, or a sheriff clerk subscribing for such as cannot write, and that before famous witnesses, betwixt and the first day of January next to come, in the presence of the Lords of our Privy Council, or the sheriffs, or their deputies, of the respective shires where any of the said persons live."

This then was the third and final demand made to the clansmen, both the Chiefs and their folk, to submit to King William and his Government. It was now the only valid and authoritative manner in which they could safeguard their lives and property. The demand made after Cromdale in May was, as far as we can find, in general terms: i.e. to submit, or take the consequences. No final date was fixed, and no officials mentioned as competent to receive that submission. Then in June came Hill's own effort to regularize the situation and he demands "a strict oath and sets a day". Both these demands (in May and June) seem to have been ignored by most of the clansmen, except some of the "middle men" or gentry. As we shall see these three separate demands to submit only caused confusion in the minds of those threatened. There was no clause in the third and final demand to show that it superseded the two previous.

The delay of the chiefs to take the oath is quite understandable. It has been attributed to stiff-necked pride on their part, and the unwillingness of any of them to be first to do so; but the real reason was that clause in their agreement by which they were to be allowed to get James' consent before submitting, an arrangement agreed to by Breadalbane on behalf of the King, as well as by King William himself. Messengers had been sent to James, and at last he gave his consent. The document is dated at St. Germain's the 12th December 1691; and the courier, a Major Menzies, did well to arrive in Dunkeld eleven days later. No wonder he was exhausted and unable to go further; but he at once sent it by express to Livingstone who was at the time at Invergarry. Menzies did his best. He knew very well he was too late to allow those far away to get their quittance from James and take the oath in time. He therefore wrote to Livingstone asking him to send the letters by express; but also to ask the

Privy Council to prorogue the time limit as it was quite impossible to reach all the chiefs. Further he added that "some persons had put the Highlanders in a bad temper!" Livingstone did present the letter to the Privy Council on January the 5th; but they told him to send it to Court, presumably for the King's attention. No more is heard of it unless the order for a general massacre which followed shortly after can be regarded as the King's reply.

As time went on and the Chiefs of Clan Cameron, Glengarry, ClanRanald, Sleat, Keppoch, Appin and Glencoe failed to make their peace, Stair became more and more impatient. The King was urging him to make an end of the matter and release the regiments tied up on garrison duty in the Highlands. He hoped Breadalbane would have completed the task of winning the Chiefs over before the time of mercy expired. In a letter to Breadalbane in December Stair begs that gentleman to get on with the work, complains that the flow of money from England had stopped, and the money already spent had done no good. To his mind the only thing to do was to root the whole lot out even before date so that no help could come to them from France, as there was still a threat that foreign aid might yet materialize. He thought that even if they took the oath it would be valueless, because they were only taking it at King James' behest; and if he allowed them to take such an oath, he could just as well absolve them from it at a later date if a fair chance of a successful rising offered. All this frustration served to increase Stair's hatred of the clans and he began plans for destroying them. Sleat was far away: ClanRanald safe in France: so the brunt would have to fall on the clans in Lochaber and the Great Glen.

As the last days of December came all the chiefs handed in their submission except Glengarry and Glencoe. The first report sent to London included MacIain in the list. Locheil and Appin went to Inveraray. Keppoch went to Inverness. Donald of Benbecula, tutor of ClanRanald, took the oath on behalf of his ward, the young Chief in France. According to the historians of Clan Donald (*Clan Donald*, Vol. 2, page 454) Alasdair Dubh of Glengarry took the oath and received pardon before the end of 1691. They do not say where he took it. Which oath did he take? The same historians say

that Keppoch took the oath on the 24th of June before
Breadalbane, Commissioner for the King! From these and
other accounts it would seem that the oaths are mixed up in
some of the records. We have seen now two oaths referred
to—the first in May after Cromdale and the second in the
official royal proclamation of August; but there appears to
have been a third demanded by Hill in June. Perhaps this was
the one taken by Keppoch on the 24th of that month? In
June Hill wrote to Melville, "Since my last the Committee of
Council and the Commander in Chief thought fit to pass
from their first strict order . . . (demanding surrender of
arms) . . . I hope I have taken a better way and easier. I sent
them a very strict oath never to take up arms against William
and his Government." He goes on to say that the Camerons
had come in and sworn, many Macdonalds of Brae Lochaber,
the Sleat gentry (but not Sir Donald), ClanRanald, and
Morar. More were coming in daily. The Appin and Glencoe
men desired to go to Argyll at Inveraray and he says, "I have
set them a short day." Who then had come in at that time,
and sworn? Surely the "middle men" or gentry of the clans,
but not the chiefs.

In the event the only valid oath was that of 29th August
1691, duly proclaimed on that day in Edinburgh. Memories
of the other oaths taken by the cadets and gentry of the clans
led MacIain to assume he could protect himself and his clan
in the same way. And yet it is plain, from all the subsequent
records, that Glengarry never did take the only valid oath
by due date. The order from the King to Hill and Livingstone
proves this, and at the same time gives Glengarry the chance
of taking it and ensuring his safety at a time sixteen full days
after due date. In addition Hill is given full powers to compromise with Alasdair Dubh of Glengarry in any way he saw
fit so long as the oath was taken in the end. The last paragraph
of the same order (see page 84) is a very different proposi-
tion. No extension of mercy or compromise here. "Delenda
est Carthago", as Stair so bluntly put it, no matter what else
may happen. Extirpation is the word used and the now
familiar "rooting out" is as good a meaning as any, in no
matter which dictionary.

Chapter Six

DECEMBER 1691

In December 1691 all was quiet in Glencoe, and indeed in Lochaber after the events of the summer. Colonel Hill's offer of an oath to the clans had been taken advantage of by many of the clansmen, notably the tacksmen and cadets whose chiefs had given permission for them to make their individual peace with the Government if they so desired. Hill had been pleased with his effort and the response to the offer he had made. The tacksmen of the Glen and their dependants dwelt in fancied security, for had they not Hill's letters of indemnity in their pockets?

At this time the total population of the Glen must have been about 500 to 600 persons, judging by the numbers of fighting men who followed Montrose and later Dundee. One can assume that the hundred men who followed Alasdair to Killiecrankie must have comprised most of the males between sixteen and sixty. There may have been some even older than sixty, for in 1745 an octogenarian was with difficulty restrained from joining MacIain's contingent. He had reached the eastern exit from the Glen before consenting to return home and look after the weaker members of the clan. Alasdair himself was over sixty in this December of 1691, and a fine figure of a warrior, over six feet tall with long hair swept back over his shoulders, moustaches and forked beard, and the physique of an athlete for all his years. He carried himself straight and proudly, and usually wore a doublet of bull-hide famous in the Highlands on account of its special mention in a writ against him and a deed of forfeiture which he had incurred for one of his raids in the eastern country of Aberdeenshire on the estate of Edinglassie. He wore tartan trews, for a chief frequently rode a shelty on his rounds, and the kilt or belted plaid was the dress of th foot soldier and huntsman. Locheil says in his *Memoirs* that MacIain "was a person of great integrity, honour, good nature and courage. He was strong and active and of the largest size, much loved by his neighbours and blameless in his conduct." He was beloved and revered by his children, not only his own but the whole family of his clan; for he was their father in the old patriarchical sense, responsible for their welfare in every way. If times were bad and crops failed, it was his burden to make things good, even if it meant, as it often did, organizing a raid on the Lowlands or the fat lands of Moray. Lady Glencoe, to give her the courtesy title accorded to the wife of a chief, was a true Macdonald too, a daughter of Archibald of Keppoch, whose large family included Coll of the Cows, the present Chief of that Clan, and several daughters, two of whom had married Campbells, strange to say. Such marriages did not always make matters better between two clans. No such complications entered here however. Coll of Keppoch and MacIain were partners in all the wild adventures of their time, as their ancestors had been before them; and one may be sure that Alasdair's wife was a loyal and devoted help-meet to her husband in all his enterprises. To her fell the task of caring for the women, children and old folk of the Glen while her husband and sons were away on their expeditions—a heavy responsibility for a woman in a temporarily defenceless glen.

At this time four cadet families of the House of Glencoe lived there, and another over the passes in Glen Etive at Dalness. In the mid-sixteenth century Ian Òg, 8th Chief of Clann Iain, had a son Ian Dubh, second of seven, whose elder brother succeeded to the Chiefship. Ian Dubh had seven sons. The eldest, Angus, succeeded his father in Dalness of Glen Etive, of which he held the tack from Campbell of Inverawe. Angus died in 1610 and was suceeded by his son, Alasdair, who escaped the Massacre and carried on the line. A hundred years later, Coll, seventh in line, took up law and became a Writer to the Signet in Edinburgh. He is famous for having successfully defended Colonel Alasdair Ranaldson Macdonell of Glengarry when he was summoned to answer for killing Captain Norman Macleod of the Black Watch in a duel. It is a pity some members of Clan Donald did not take up law earlier in their history. It might have helped them to keep a hold on their patrimony, which was so often lost through their enemies using a mixture of law and artifice.

The next sons of Ian Dubh were Ranald of the Shield and his brother, Angus (Aonghas Mac Ailein Duibh). Ranald was the hero of the exploit in Montrose's War already recounted; and Angus was the guide who led the raiding army into Campbell strongholds in the winter of 1644/45. Ranald and his son of the same name were victims of the Massacre; but Ranald Òg's two sons escaped by being from home at the time. They lived to serve in Prince Charles Edward's army in 1745. The elder, Donald, was an accomplished bard and his songs, light-hearted and satirical, were popular in the Glen for long. Ranald of the Shield had the tack (or lease) of lands in the Laroch Glen, about a mile from the main village of Carnoch, the headquarters of the Chief.

Another son of Ian Dubh, Alasdair, founded the family of Achtriochtan, and it was his grandson, John, who fell in the Massacre. John had a brother who escaped, and his grandson was one of the few Highlanders to fall at the battle of Prestonpans in '45.

Two more sons of Ian Dubh, Ian Òg and Ian Mòr, founded the families of Inverigan and Achnacon respectively. The links between them and the representatives of these two families at the time of the Massacre are lost. Even their Christian names are unknown. They are simply referred to in all letters and documents as "Inverigan" and "Achnacon" in the accepted mode of referring to a gentleman by the name of his lands.

As one comes along the shore road from the ferry of Ballachulish the first settlement of the Clann Iain is in Laroch Glen, home of Ranald of the targe, looking out to Eilean Munde, the burial isle in the loch. A mile further on is the mouth of the Glen; and, where the river runs into Loch Leven, the largest of the settlements and the Chief's own house at Invercoe (now a a ruin and scarcely traceable). The village is Carnoch and in 1691 did not contain very many houses. The Gaels never seemed to build large villages or towns. They preferred to live in scattered hamlets from end to end

of a strath or glen. This distribution of the population proved
a blessing when the murderers tried to blot the whole community out in one blow. Accurate timing was essential to the
success of the plan; and, when that broke down, avenues of
escape were left open. A mile up the glen from Carnoch one
comes to Inverigan (Inbhir Fhiodhan) at the confluence of
the Rigan Burn (Allt Fhiodhan) with the main stream. About
a mile farther up on the right bank of the river is Leac an
Tuim (now a Youth Hostel), and another mile south, in a
bend in the river and under the shadow of the Signal Rock,
Achnacon (Achadh nan Con—Field of the Hounds), with
Clachaig on the other side of the river. Thereafter the glen
takes its turn eastwards and a mile and a half upstream is
Loch Triochtan with Achnambeithe (Achadh nam Beithe—
Birch Tree Field) at its lower end and Achtriochtan, a small
hamlet at the upper end of the loch, where traces of the
houses burned by the soldiers are still to be seen. Beyond this
point the glen becomes very narrow and there was little
settlement of a permanent nature, only the sheiling bothies
where the dairymaids lived while the cattle grazed on the
summer pastures (*airighean*). Here butter and cheese were
made and stored in butts for the winter stocks. These sheilings
went far up to the borders of Rannoch Moor; but were of
course occupied only in summer.

The wastes of the Rannoch Moor, wild enough today, were
in those days a veritable wilderness with some remains of the
old Caledonian forest still extant, where wild life lived in
abundance. In spite of the attentions of hunters like Donald
MacDonald (Domhnall Mac Fhionnlaigh nan Dan—Donald
Mac Finlay of the Songs), who flourished in the early part of
the sixteenth century, wolves were still a menace. Donald, a
Glencoe man, who was a skilful archer, had nearly cleared
the wolves out of the Brae Lochaber and Loch Treig district;
but some still lingered on in the Highlands till the early
eighteenth century, when the last fell to the brave attack of a
woman in Strath Glass. Cameron of Locheil and a woman in
Badenoch are also mentioned as the slayers of the last wolf in
Scotland. The reindeer, elk, beaver, boar and wild ponies had
gone by this time; but red deer, roe, eagles, kites, buzzards
and ravens abounded. Wild goats too lived on the higher

ground away from the swampy flats, as they still do in some
parts of the Highlands to this day. Life in these sheilings,
which were the equivalent of the "setrs" of Norway, is
described vividly in an old poem composed by a young girl
to her lover. This poetess was, judging from internal evidence
in the poem, a Glencoe girl. She describes the clothes and
finery he would bring her from the towns on his return from
the cattle-droving in the south, and adds a significant verse
asking, "Why should we lack for anything while the Lowlanders have cattle? We would get cattle from Moray and
sheep from the low country." (*Bardachd Gaidhlig*—Watson,
1918.) The Glencoe sheilings with their rough and ready
bothies for the shelter of the dairymaids would be on the
edge of this wild country, and the young men frequently
visited them for courtship, and also for defence against the
attacks of wolves and other predators, human as well as
others.

Returning to Achnacon there is a side glen running almost
due south—Gleann na Lice Muidhe (The Glen of the Flag-
stone of the Churn). In this glen was a farm belonging to
MacIain where he was supposed to have been living at this
time. There are here the ruins of a fairly considerable settlement. The name of the glen indicates that it played an important part in the dairying activities of the community.

In winter the people were more concentrated than at any
other time of the year. Achtriochtan being higher up the
glen than any other hamlet was almost deserted. The tacks-
man himself was staying at Achnacon, leaving only a few
retainers on his farm. The chief's sons were living at Carnoch; and it would seem that Alasdair and his lady had left
their big house to John, their eldest son, who was in any
case soon to inherit the chiefship and who took some of
the responsibility of the position off his father's shoulders.
Alasdair, the younger brother, had married Elspeth Stewart
of Ardsheal, and they were living not far from John. Much
has been said about the fact that Glenlyon was related to
young Alasdair. The relationship was in fact fairly distant.
Elspeth's grandfather, Duncan Stewart of Ardsheal, had
married (as her third husband) Jean Campbell, daughter of
Sir Robert Campbell of Glenurchy. By her first husband,

Archibald Campbell of Glenlyon, she had Robert Campbell, Captain in Argyll's Regiment, and Laird of Glenlyon. So Alasdair's wife was, one might say, Glenlyon's niece; and Alasdair in a very distant way, Glenlyon's nephew.

The two brothers, John and Alasdair, were living near to each other at Carnoch this winter. The rest of their people were in the various hamlets throughout the lower reaches of the glen between Signal Rock and the sea, the best part in which to pass the winter, low-lying and sheltered.

December drew to a close. On the 29th MacIain at last received the long awaited news from King James that he was free to take the oath and safeguard his clan from the wrath of King William. He was the last to receive Livingstone's express letter. Locheil, Appin, Keppoch and ClanRanald's Tutor had all taken the oath with little time to spare. So he set out with confidence to reach Inverlochy before the sands ran out. He had no doubt but that Hill would swear him in and all would be well. He arrived at the Fort to find it crowded with troops, Hill's own regiment and some 400 men of Argyll's Regiment, the rest of which were disposed in various strategic spots. One company under Drummond, of evil memory, was at Barcaldine to overawe the Appin Stewarts. Hill received him kindly, as was his wont. He had a sort of private admiration for the proud old man. When MacIain asked for the oath to be administered, indicating his desire to have the distasteful formality over and done with, Hill shocked him by announcing that it was outside his power to do it, pointing out the clause in the August Proclamation that the oath was to be taken before the Sheriffs of the shires in which the applicants resided. MacIain remarked that Hill had given Achtriochtan and Achnacon his blessing and a letter to protect them. Hill could only state that that had been a previous oath of his own making, but the fact remained that now, as at this date, he must appear before the Sheriff of his shire and swear it in his presence. MacIain was dumbfounded. All his efforts had been in vain. He had waited overlong for King James' quittance; and now, at near midnight on the 29th/30th he was a good fifteen miles on the wrong side of his glen and must needs retrace his steps and get to Inveraray before midnight of the 31st, a journey

of over sixty miles, impossible even in good weather. To
make matters worse the wind was in the north and it was
obvious that snow was on its way. Waiting only long enough
to beg a letter from Hill to the Sheriff stating the circumstances he set out once more. By dawn he had crossed Loch
Leven and taken the shore road through the Lettermore and
Kintalen, past Duror. Short cuts in the blizzards threatening
were out of the question. He must make as much speed as
possible.

In Appin ill luck befell him. Passing, as he was forced to
do, near to Barcaldine some soldiers of Argyll's Regiment
arrested him and his gillie and took them before Captain
Drummond, who would have liked to have thrown him into
prison for life; but, in the circumstances, had to content
himself with locking him up in a cell for the night. Colonel
Hill's letter protected him; but it was a sad Hogmanay for
the old man, and his thoughts were not much on the con-
viviality of the occasion. A sadder man set out next morning.
It was the 1st of January and the time had expired. He was
now very much on the wrong side of the law. However, there
was nothing for it but to try his luck with the Sheriff at
Inveraray. Crossing Loch Etive at Bonawe he spent the night
at Taynuilt, and managed to reach Inveraray on the 2nd of
the month. Here again his fortune seemed to have run right
out. The Sheriff of Argyll, Campbell of Ardkinglas, was away
from home, visiting his home and relatives during the New
Year celebrations. Ardkinglas was an honest man, and as well
liked by MacIain as any Campbell could be. But here he was
now in an unfriendly town, obliged to await the return of the
Sheriff. At last, on the 5th Ardkinglas arrived full of good
cheer and in jovial mood. MacIain approached him with the
request that he administer the oath and let him go home. The
Sheriff told him he was five days too late and nothing could be
done. To the old man's entreaties he replied he would think
it over and would see him next day. No doubt he read and
re-read Hill's letter in which the colonel begged him to
receive this "great lost sheep" into the fold, and do his best
for him. On the morning of the 6th MacIain duly presented
himself. Ardkinglas gave him the oath and promised to
forward it at once to the Council in Edinburgh. He kept his

word; and the Chief light-heartedly set out for home, feeling
secure that he had put himself and his children under the
protection of the law after all.

The oath taken by MacIain and duly certified by the Sheriff
was sent to Colin Campbell, Sheriff Clerk of Argyll, who was
in Edinburgh at this time, together with a letter stating how
earnest the chief had been, enclosing Hill's letter, and asking
that all three be presented to the Privy Council at the earliest
opportunity. He even asked Colin to report to him at once
the action taken. Campbell obeyed and showed them all to the
Clerks of the Council, Sir Gilbert Elliot and David Moncreiff.
They were in a quandary, but on a point of law would have
nothing to do with the matter. The Sheriff Clerk then tried a
number of Privy Councillors, one of whom was Lord Stair,
father of the Master. They objected, and the matter was
referred to Lord Aberuchill, another Campbell. In the end it
was decided to cancel it and hand it to the Clerk of Council.
It was never presented to the whole Council in session. Of
course, legally they were right; but the Royal Commission,
which reported later on the matter, blamed them all for not
bringing all three documents before the full Council as
requested by the Sheriff of Argyll.

So the oath was null and void; but MacIain back at home
was ignorant of that fact. He trusted that the genial Ardkinglas would do his best for him. On his return he told his
clan that all was well and they could dwell in peace; but
advised his tacksmen to make sure of their safety by following
his example at the first opportunity. They never did, as far
as written records show, nor is it likely that they had time
to do so before disaster fell upon them.

A great relief settled on them all, and life resumed its
normal winter routine. Meantime, all unknown to them,
things were happening in London and Edinburgh which
were to bring death in its most treacherous form into their
beautiful valley.

Chapter Seven

AGENDA FOR SLAUGHTER

JANUARY came in. Stair was in London awaiting news from Scotland. Meantime he wrote letters. In 1691 his threats and Breadalbane's bribes had all failed. It only remained now to see if the chiefs would take the oath and make their peace. But he had not left the formulation of plans till now. He was a very thorough gentleman and as early as the 3rd December he had written to Hamilton showing his especial rage against Clan Donald in all its branches. He wrote: "The Macdonalds will fall into the net. That's the only Popish clan in the kingdom and it will be popular to take severe course with them. Let me hear from you whether you think this is the proper season to maul them in the long cold nights, and what force will be necessary to your garrison and the Regiment of Leven which is at Inverness, whether dragoons can subsist any time 10 or 12 miles from Invergarry, to be on hand if any occasion require, and if your being provided with a petard or some cannon may not easily be master of Invergarry." So there was the net, planned beforehand for the Macdonalds to fall into. On the 7th January he wrote to Livingstone: "The troops at Inverness and Inverlochy will be ordered to take the house of Invergarry, and destroy entirely the country of Lochaber, Locheil's lands, Keppoch's, Glengarry's, Appin and Glencoe. . . . I assure you your power shall be full enough, and I hope the soldiers will not trouble the Government with prisoners. . . . It's true, it's a rigid season for the soldiers to work, but it's the only time they cannot escape you, for human constitutions cannot endure to be long out of houses. A few days will do all that's at present either necessary or possible." That was his grand plan. His hate seems to have blinded him to the fact that to utterly

81

destroy an area as wide as that envisaged, with the troops at his disposal, was well nigh impossible. At the time this was written it would seem he had not heard of the oaths taken by Locheil, Keppoch and Appin, although these had done so in time. Timing is here important.

Letters by "flying packet" could be sent and an answer received between Edinburgh and London in eight days. Allowing two or three days for mails from the more distant parts of the Highlands to reach Edinburgh, it is scarcely possible that Stair knew that some of the chiefs had in fact taken the oath within the due date. He would surely have made some mention of this fact in that letter had he known. No, the plan was made in anticipation, and indeed in the pious hope, that the Chiefs would not after all conform in time.

In the letter of 3rd December he makes one of the few mentions of the fact that religion came into the matter at all. It is true that most of the clans engaged with Dundee were Roman Catholics; but they were not bigoted. In fact before the end of 1691 Hill wrote that Keppoch averred he was a Protestant. They stood much firmer on the ground of loyalty to their rightful King than on any matters of religious faith. It is strange that, as the "Glorious Revolution" was regarded by the Protestants as a great triumph over Popery, more mention is not made in all the letters written at this time to the fact that some of the clans were Papists. Stair states that the Macdonalds were the "only Popish clan in the kingdom"; but, if this were true, why plan to destroy Locheil and Appin as well? It is quite clear that religion entered very little into the hate which had its expression in the Massacre. The King himself had, it will be remembered, expressly stated in his coronation oath that there was to be no religious persecution after his accession. Stair too was not very biased in the matter of creeds. In fact he was tolerant. After all he had held high office under a Catholic sovereign before William arrived.

By the 9th Stair must have heard the first report that all had submitted for he at once wrote to Livingstone: "I could have wished the Macdonalds had not divided, and I am sorry Keppoch and Glencoe are safe." On the 11th Argyll told him he had received an express letter from Ardkinglas reporting that Glencoe had taken the oath too late, and the action he had taken to forward all the documents to Edinburgh for the attention of the Council. He could not have known then that these had never been presented to the Privy Council in session; nor that they had been deleted from the records. In time he heard, from his father who knew about the transaction even if he did not take part in it, that the oath was null and void in the eyes of the negotiators in Edinburgh. On the same day as he received this news, Stair wrote to Livingstone: "Argyll tells me that Glencoe hath not taken the oath at which I rejoice."

Between this date and the 16th there was much consultation between the King and Stair, with Breadalbane on call for advice about tactics, as his special knowledge of the terrain was of great value to those who knew little about the Glen and its surroundings. The result of their deliberations appeared on the 16th in the form of explicit orders from the King to the Commander in Chief, Livingstone, a copy of which was sent to Colonel Hill at Inverlochy.

(From the Culloden Papers, being originals in possession of Duncan George Forbes of Culloden)

Orders upon which the Massacre of Glencoe proceeded by which thirty-eight persons lost their lives.

Instructions from the King to Colonel Hill
16 Jany. 1692

William R.

1. The copy of the paper given by Macdonald of Aughtera to you hath been shewn to us. We did formerly grant passes to Buchan and Cannon, and we do authorise and allow you to grant passes to them, and ten servants to each of them, to come freely and safely to Leith; from that to be transported to the Netherlands before the 15th March next, to go from then where they please, without any stop or trouble.

2. We doe allow you to receive the submission of Glengarry and those with him, upon their taking the oath of allegiance and delivering up the house of Invergarry, to be safe as to their lives, but as to their estates to depend on our mercy.

3. In case ye find that the house of Invergarry cannot probably be taken in this season of the year, with the artillery and provision ye can bring there; in that case we leave it to your discretion to give Glengarry an assurance of the entire indemnity for life and fortune, upon delivery of the house and arms, and taking the oath of alledgiance. In this you are to act as you find the circumstances of the affair do require; but it were better that those who have not taken the benefit of our indemnity, in the terms within the diet prefixt by our proclamation, should be obliged to render upon mercy. The taking of the oath is indispensible, others having already taken it.

4. If M'Ean of Glenco and that tribe can well be separated from the rest, it will be a proper vindication of public Justice to extirpate that sect of thieves. The double of these instructions is only communicated to Sir Thomas Livingstone.

W.R.

It is to be noted that the King both superscribes and subscribes this document, and much has been said about this meaning to indicate that William made very sure of the order to annihilate the men of Glencoe. Some do not regard this double signature as anything out of the ordinary. Other cases of the same procedure are quoted. (See Appendix III.)

The date is said to be in Stair's hand; and in the Memoir of Sir James Dalrymple it is stated that it is written "in language which there is little doubt is that of the Master of Stair". There can be no doubt but that the order was inspired, even if not written, by Stair himself.

As we have seen already, this order expressly allows a means of escape for Glengarry even although he had not yet taken the oath; and designates Glencoe for extirpation. As if this double transmission of the order were not enough, the Master of Stair wrote on the same day to the Commander in Chief emphasizing the importance of making Glencoe a "just example of vengeance".

In this Order the parts played by the King and Stair in the planning of the Massacre are clearly seen. Breadalbane's share is not so obvious. However, he was in London at the time and he alone of the three had the necessary knowledge of the Highlands, and that part of them in particular, to advise how best to compass the trapping of the MacIains in their stronghold. Hill could have told them; but it seems from all the letters written at this time that the King and Stair preferred to deal with Livingstone direct, which is quite understandable; and Livingstone with Lt.-Colonel Hamilton, which is not quite so easy to accept. After all Hamilton was Hill's subordinate, and yet we find later orders of a vital nature going direct to Hamilton. The powers seemed to suspect that Hill was partial towards the Highlanders. Perhaps he was at this time. Later we shall have to examine his conduct.

In a much earlier letter to Breadalbane the Master of Stair had referred to "your" plan for "mauling the rebels", as if it were Breadalbane's own idea, which no doubt it was, although apart from circumstantial evidence of this kind it is hard to pin it on him. But then it was very hard to prove anything against him. He kept his tracks well covered up when he had a mind to. He even managed to get out of the suspicion of double-dealing occasioned by the exposure of the private articles agreed at the meeting at Achachallader, which was quite an achievement. From this time (January 1692) his part in the plots and execution of the Massacre is shrouded in mystery. Here and there, however, we find a pointer, and one such soon emerges; as, following on the King's order, the plans of the Royal minions mature.

Stair sent a copy of the King's orders to Hill by the same post by which Livingstone received his, presumably to make sure somebody got them. With them he sent a letter similar to that sent to the Commander in Chief, but containing the following enlightening paragraph. "The Earls of Argyle and Breadalbane have promised that they (the MacIains) shall have no retreat in their bounds, the passes to Rannoch would be secured, and the hazard certified to the Laird of Weem (Menzies) to reset them; in that case Argyle's detachment with a party that may be posted in Island Stalker must cut them off." Here is abundant proof that both Argyll and Breadalbane were in the plot, and Menzies too, though the latter acted under duress, if indeed he was obliged to act at all. He was after all one of Breadalbane's protégés. It cannot be argued that the two Campbell Earls thought that this was just another of those harrying expeditions accompanied by the burning of houses and driving of cattle. It was plainly a plan for the complete cutting off of the whole clan. Escape routes far away were to be guarded—Rannoch, Glen Etive, Glen Dochart, and all the possible ways to the South which lay in the Campbell lands. Castle Stalker guarded Appin and overawed the Stewarts there. In the event we shall see how effective these dispositions were; but it seemed that nothing had been left to chance and there could be no possible ecape for the unfortunate Clan Iain of Glencoe.

On the 23rd January Livingstone wrote to Lt.-Colonel Hamilton at Fort William. Hamilton was Hill's Lt.-Colonel actually, although he is addressed here as "Colonel" for some reason.

Sir Thomas Livingstone, Commander in Chief in Scotland,
to Coll. Hamilton at Fort William.

Sir, Since my last I understand that the Laird of Glenco, coming after the prefixed time, was not admitted to take the oath, which is very good news here, being that at Court it's wished he had not taken it, so that that thieving nest might be entirely rooted out, for the Secretary in three of his last letters hath made mention of him, and it is known at Court he has not taken it. So, Sir, here is a fair occasion for you to show that your garrison serves for some use; and being that the orders are so positive from Court to me not to spare any of them that have not timely come in, as you may by the orders I sent your colonel, I desire you would begin with Glenco, and spair nothing which belongs to him, but do not trouble the Government with prisoners. I shall expect to hear what progress you have made in this, and remain, Sir,

Your humble servant,

T. Livingstone.

This was one case of the higher powers going behind Hill's back in their orders. It is interesting to note that the "Court" wished MacIain had not taken the oath so that he might be entirely rooted out. Surely, the "Court" referred to must have included the King?

On the 30th January Stair again wrote to Livingstone

telling him that the job must be done thoroughly or not at all, as it would be useless to harry the clan and make them more intransigent. They must be cut off utterly. To Hill he also wrote that all must be "secret and sudden", but giving no details of the manner in which it must be carried out, although at this time the orders must have gone out to Glenlyon to march into the Glen. One would like to believe that Hill was not kept "in the picture" because he was suspected of being an unwilling participant in the plot.

By the end of the month the arrangements were complete. Major Duncanson, with his second in Command, Captain Drummond, had brought his company of Argyll's Regiment up to Ballachulish, thus holding the shore road to Appin, close to the scene of action. The Fort at Inverlochy was full of troops to the number of 800, 400 from Hill's Regiment and a similar number of Argyll's. Indeed it was overcrowded, and that was the excuse given for moving a company of Argyll's to Glencoe for quartering. The passes South were held. Hamilton could move unnoticed to Kinlochleven at any time, thence by the old military road over the Devil's Staircase into the headwaters of the Glen. His was the hardest task of all if he were to arrive with his troops fit for action after the gruelling climb over the Staircase in the weather prevailing. However, he had time on his side, if he cared to set out early enough, for his movements were unlikely to be perceived by any of the inhabitants of Glencoe.

There remained only one detail to attend to in order to make the whole scheme a resounding success. That essential factor was surprise. This was to be provided in the base and treacherous manner which has made the Massacre of Glencoe the most notorious crime in Scottish history, out of all proportion to the number of victims slaughtered. Many other murders have been committed in our nation's long history in which many times the number of men, women and children met their death; and yet these are seldom remembered while Glencoe has never been forgotten.

Chapter Eight

MASSACRE

On the morning of the 1st February a company of soldiers was marching along the shore road from Ballachulish towards the mouth of the Glen. It was at once seen and reported to MacIain, who immediately sent word to his clansmen to hide their weapons, and called his sons to his side. After a short consultation it was decided that John and Alasdair Òg should take a party of twenty men and meet the troops to find out as soon as possible their intentions. As the two young men got nearer they saw it was a company of Argyll's Regiment with a Captain, a Lieutenant and an Ensign at their head. Very soon they recognized the Captain commanding the company to be Robert Campbell of Glenlyon, uncle of Alasdair's wife. None too pleased to have a Campbell coming to their glen, they nonetheless were somewhat relieved that he was at any rate a connection by marriage, even if not a blood relation. Surely he could mean no harm.

Glenlyon, a cadet of the House of Breadalbane, was a robust hearty man of sixty years of age. He was handsome in a rather effeminate way with a weak mouth, pointed chin and the complexion of one accustomed to convivial living. In his younger days he had achieved quite a reputation for his addiction to cards and the bottle. In 1680 he had been with Glenurchy on his raid into Caithness at Allt nam Meirleach. After that he had led a quieter life; but his habits got him into debt even for the necessities of life. At one time there were writs out against him for the purchase of meal, which his son-in-law, Campbell of Ardeonaig, had to pay for him. The raid of 1689 already referred to quite crippled him financially, and he was glad to take a commission in the newly raised Regiment of Argyll, although the rank of Captain was not quite what he would have aspired to in the ordinary way. If the excursion by Keppoch and MacIain through his lands after Killiecrankie cost him only a part of the £7,500, assessed as the proceeds of that raid, one can well imagine that he had no great love for MacIain and his clan.

With Glenlyon marched his two subalterns, Lieutenant Lindsay, a relative of Glenlyon's wife, and Ensign Lundie. The latter is called also Lindsay in some accounts, but the muster rolls do not reveal a second officer of that name in this company, while there is an Ensign Lundie in another company in October 1691. It may be that the younger Lindsay joined the Regiment between October and February. The soldiers in the company were not all Highlanders, but there was a good number of Campbells or their associated clans. The rest bear Lowland names. One other member of the detachment, and a very important one, was Sergeant Barbour, an Englishman. Judging by the position of trust given to him he acted almost like a Company Sergeant-Major. Perhaps he was a regular soldier attached for training purposes, like the Permanent Staff Instructors in our modern Territorial Army. These then were the men who took the leading part in the actual murders committed in the Glen. These are the names remembered by anyone who has read even the briefest accounts of the transactions of the 13th February 1692. (See Appendix IV.)

John and Alasdair MacIain greeted Glenlyon politely and asked him his business. Glenlyon was very cordial and almost apologetic. Calling up his Lieutenant he asked him for the written orders he had received from his commander. They were billeting orders commanding the MacIains to house and feed the company, as there was no room for them in the fort of Inverlochy. An additional reason given was that they had come to collect arrears of cess and hearth money, a new tax imposed in 1690. The three officers gave their paroles of honour that they came with no hostile intentions. In spite of the obvious inconvenience of having a company of hungry soldiers to house and feed in a glen already quite densely populated, and with their supplies of winter food running low daily, the young men told Glenlyon he was welcome and his party would have hospitality for as long as they had to stay.

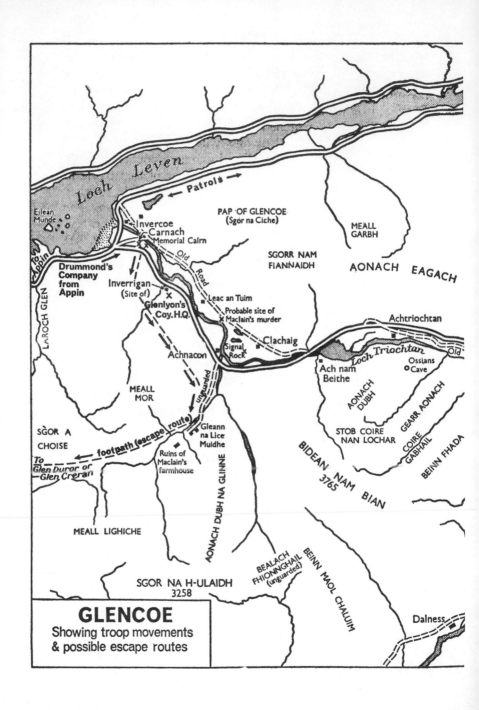

GLENCOE

Showing troop movements
& possible escape routes

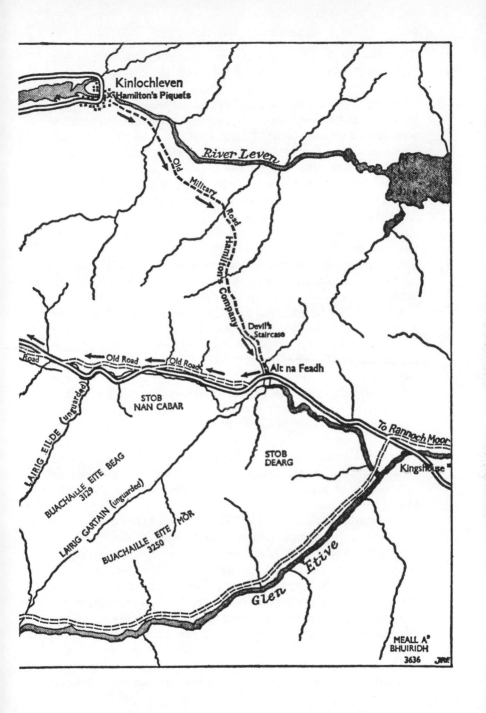

The demeanour of their guest was friendly and cordial; in fact he seemed to be quite a decent fellow to all outward appearances, whatever may have been going on in his mind at the time. At this time he had no certain knowledge of the part he was going to be ordered to play, or even that a massacre was contemplated. In all fairness one has to assume this. He was, after all, a junior officer, and the plotters had been told that what was to be done must be done secretly and suddenly. Captains and subalterns might well have been left out of the secret until the last moment when there would be little chance of their backing out. The reasons for his being sent to Glencoe were plausible enough for a simple soldier. One can hardly imagine that anyone could have lived as a guest in another's house for a fortnight with such a heavy load on his mind, and not have given away some of his inner thoughts.

With lighter hearts, and their fears somewhat allayed, the young men joined the company and took Glenlyon and his officers to their father who met them with due dignity and friendship, confirming the promises of full hospitality given by his sons. The old Chief did not at any time seem to have any hesitation in accepting the assurances of Glenlyon that the visit was an entirely friendly one, and that no harm of any kind was meant towards him or his clan. Ian Òg, the eldest son, was quite happy about it all. Not so Alasdair. He from the beginning seems to have had his doubts, and it was well that he had, as things turned out. If he had been as complaisant as his father and brother there is no saying what might have been the result.

The visitors settled down. Glenlyon and his officers chose to lodge at Inverigan, which is just about in the centre of habitation. From that point he could be in touch with his detachments scattered among the houses of the clan. Sergeant Barbour was sent to Achnacon. The Macdonalds farthest away from these concentrations were the few caretakers on the farm at Achtriochtan and the farm workers up at Gleann Muidhe on MacIain's own farm.

The soldiers to the number of sixty, according to the muster roll of October '91 (q.v.), but according to other accounts 120, were distributed, three or four to a house,

among the indwellers of the Glen, so that every house was
under guard of their guests, who could be ready at any hour
of the night or day to carry out their orders. These orders
were not, of course, cummunicated to the troops until a few
hours before Zero Hour. In the meantime soldiers and clansmen lived together at close quarters under the same roof,
sharing the same beds and board, like one family. The
quarters must indeed have been very close, considering sixty
soldiers (at the least) were living in a community of some
500 to 600 souls, already concentrated in their winter
quarters.

The weather, so unkind to MacIain on his journey to
Inveraray, had now moderated, and was almost spring-like.
The activities of the people included all the usual work and
play of a Highland community. As night fell there were
ceilidhs in the houses, with music, games and story-telling
to pass the long evenings. In all these the guests took part.
Soldiers soon settle down to the changed life of billets after
the stark conditions of barrack life; and these men of Argyll's
Regiment had just come from a crowded fort. Their life here
in Glencoe must have been very much happier than they
had experienced for long. It was inevitable that friendships
were made, and perhaps even the beginnings of some love
affairs. At this time the only daughter we know of in old
MacIain's family was in the Glen and her continual com-
panions were the two daughters of Achtriochtan. The three
girls were of much the same age—from seventeen to nineteen
years old. Owing to the very unwelcome attentions forced
upon them by some of the soldiers they were sent away to
the farm in Glen Muidhe for safety. This would seem to
indicate that there were some responsible relatives up there;
and these, or most of them, were in a good position later to
join the escaping party organized by the young MacIains. At
any rate the girls were not resident with their parents after
Glenlyon's arrival. As the first misgivings died away under
the continued peace and apparent good-will of the visitors
the people of the Glen settled down to life as usual, doing
their best to entertain their guests with the scanty supplies at
their disposal; and so life went on for nearly a fortnight until
the evening of the 12th February.

Reputed site of MacIain's house in Gleann na Lice Muidhe with slab bearing a memorial to MacIain's death.

No troops had been billeted on MacIain and his lady. It would have been too obvious, and scarcely in keeping with the spirit of friendship to keep them under such close surveillance. In any case it was a wise move, if one wishes to look for motives, to leave the Chief and his lady to the privacy of their own house. Where that house was at this time is a matter of some difference of opinion. His main "manor-house" was at Carnoch near the site of the present house of Invercoe at the bridge over the river on the road to Kinlochleven. This house was erected the year before the Massacre, and the gable-end stood until a great storm during the last century blew it down. In front of the house was a great tree known as the "Giant of the Forest" which was destroyed by the same storm. This was taken as an omen of the passing of the estate into other hands. This information is given by a lineal descendant of the MacIain family. The elder son, John, was in this house at this time, and his brother not far away in Carnoch. The Chief must have been elsewhere. The site generally accepted is the farm-house a mile and a half from Achnacon up in Gleann Muidhe. On the hillside above the sheep-folds of the present farm is the ruined foundation of a fairly large house with two apartments and a gable-end with a fireplace at each end of it. There is also a small outhouse on the east gable sufficient for a fuel-store or byre for a cow. This is the site on which is erected a memorial slab, stating that it was here that MacIain was murdered. Even here there are two possible sites of his house. Seton Gordon, whose knowledge of Highland history is profound, in his book *Highways and Byways in the Western Highlands*, says the site has been covered by rubble from the stream near which it stood, although the hearth-stone was visible some years ago. This description does not fit the other ruin which is well away from the stream and still very well defined. Dr. I. F. Grant, M.B.E., LL.D., the well-known expert on Highland history and customs, is of opinion that the large house on which the slab is erected is too spacious, and the style of building does not fit the period, especially as it was only a secondary farmhouse of the Chief, who was not in any case a wealthy man. Of these two sites in Gleann Muidhe it is very hard to decide which was MacIain's especially as one of them has now disappeared.

The descendant of MacIain already referred to above states that many years ago he visited the site of MacIain's residence at the time of the Massacre. It was shown him by two old men of good repute, whose knowledge of the traditions of the Glen was "quite amazing". From his description the ruins lay in a wood about half way between Clachaig and Leac an Tuim. Even at that time they needed spades to uncover the remains of the walls, and no idea of the size and shape of the house could be got. This site, in the middle of the habitation in the most sheltered part of the Glen, seems to be a much more likely place for the Chief to pass the winter than far away from his folk up a side glen. Further, as we shall see. the actions of the chief's sons during that anxious night, when they (according to one account) were able to consult their father about the unusual troop movements going on, and yet return to their own houses and visit Glenlyon at Innerigan, all seem to point to the fact that the houses occupied by the father and his sons could not have been so far apart. It would have been impossible to get up to Gleann Muidhe and back in the time at their disposal. On the whole we incline to the belief that MacIain's house, the site of his death, was in the main glen midway between Achnacon and Carnoch; but exactly where it is now impossible to determine.

This then was the disposition of the actors in the tragedy about to be enacted. On the 12th three letters were sent out.

1.   Colonel Hill to Hamilton

Ft. William 12 Feb. 1692

Sir, You are, with 400 men of my regt., and the 400 of my lord Argyll's Regt. under command of Major Duncanson, to march straight to Glenco, and there put into due execution the orders you have received from the Commander in Chief.

Given under my hand at Fort William 12th Feb.

[*sic sub*] John Hill.

This letter is the only document incriminating Hill; and it may be said that he did not know all that the orders received from the Commander in Chief implied, as Hamilton's orders were sent to him direct from Livingstone. At this time Hamilton seems to have been at Ballachulish with Duncanson, although it is unlikely his own detachment destined to cross the Devil's Staircase were there. His letter, which follows, is headed "Ballachulish", so perhaps his troops were on the north side of the ferry, whence they would have to march round by the head of the Loch, over the Staircase and into Glencoe. No wonder they were late.

2.   Hamilton to Duncanson

Ballechyllis 12 Feby. 1692

Sir, Persuant to the Commander in Chief's and my Colonel's order to me for putting into execution the King's command, you are to order your affair so, as that the several posts already assigned you by you and your several detachments fall in activeness precisely by five of the clock tomorrow morning, being Saturday; at which time I will endeavour the same with those appointed from this regiment for the other places. It will be most necessary you secure those avenues on the south side, that the old fox, nor none of his cubs get away. The orders are that none be spared from seventy, of the sword, nor the Government troubled with prisoners. This all until I see you.

From your humble servant,

James Hamilton.

"The Highland Wedding" by J. de Witt, showing the dress of ordinary people of the late seventeenth century (*by courtesy of* Sir John Clerk of Penicuik, Bart.; *photo*: National Galleries of Scotland).

The Upper Glen looking down to Achtriochtan from below gorge; Aonach Dubh and Gearr Aonach on left, Aonach Eagach on right (*photo*: John Leng, Dundee).

Please to order a guard to secure the ferry, and the boats
there, and the boats must be all on this side the ferry, after
your men are over.

For Their Majesties' service, for Major Duncanson
of the Earl of Argyll's Regiment.

From this letter it is patent that the posts assigned to the
various detachments, and the part to be played by Glenlyon's
company, had all been thought out some days before. The
instructions, too, become more explicit. All under seventy
are to be killed, and the Chief must not escape.

3.   Duncanson to Glenlyon

12 Feby. 1692

Sir, You are hereby ordered to fall upon the rebells the
Macdonalds of Glenco and put all to the sword under
seventy. You are to have special care that the old fox and his
sons do not escape your hands; you are to secure all avenues,
that no man escape. This you are to put in execution at five
of the clock precisely; and by that time, or very shortly after
it, I will strive to be at you with a stronger party. If I do not
come to you at five, you are not to tarry for me, but to fall on.
This is by the King's special commands, for the good and
safety of the Countrey, that these miscreants be cut off root
and branch. See that this be put in execution without fear or
favour, or you may expect to be dealt with as one not true
to King or Government, nor a man fit to carry a commission
in the King's service. Expecting you will not fail in the
fulfilling hereof, as you love yourself, I subscribe this at
Ballychyllis, the 12 Feby. 1692.

Robert Duncanson.

This, the final written instruction, is the most virulent of all.
The orders to spare none under seventy and to see that the
Chief and his sons do not escape are repeated with emphasis.
Then, to make sure, a threat which could hardly be more
menacing, is added. It appears they were not too sure of
Glenlyon.

Evening came. Glenlyon and his officers had made their
usual visits during the day to take the morning draught
with MacIain and his sons. They had accepted the Chief's

7

invitation to dinner on the following night, and all seemed quite peaceful and friendly. The two young MacIains were at Inverigan spending the evening with Glenlyon playing cards. Between six and seven o'clock a runner arrived with a despatch for Campbell—the letter quoted above. It could be seen at once by his face that Glenlyon was taken aback by this interruption. To the anxious inquiries of the young men he replied lightly that a soldier never knew what was to happen next; but he would have to ask them to stop the game as he had work to do. He made the excuse that there was trouble up the way of Glengarry and he had been called out, to prepare to move. Even he could hardly continue to play a game of cards with his intended victims and a letter like that lying in his pocket. John and Alasdair left him to his thoughts. One can picture the worried captain sitting by the fire reading and re-reading his orders, and especially the last paragraph and the threats contained therein. We must assume

In 1899 this cup was in possession of Captain Duncan Cameron MacDonald of Glencoe, and the tradition connected with it states that it is a sixteenth-century French cup, brought back from Paris by MacIain in his youth. He used it to pledge his foes the night before the Massacre; and, when the survivors returned later it was found among the ashes of his house. This cup, however, is more likely to be of Scots manufacture, as a similar cup, exhibited in Edinburgh in 1951 at the Living Traditions Festival Exhibition of Scottish Crafts and called a "Thistle Cup", was made by Alexander Forbes of Edinburgh c. 1692.

that the whole bloody business was distasteful to any human being; but he had his orders and had to make up his mind. He decided to see it through. He could hardly summon his officers to the billet where Inverigan and his family might overhear his conversations with Lindsay, the Ensign and Barbour. He must have gone aside to some post where no indwellers were at hand. His officers took their orders without question. How the orders were received by the rest of the company is a matter for conjecture. No dissentient in this company is recorded in the Inquiry, although it takes notice of the two in Hamilton's company. One may assume that none refused duty openly. There is a story that one soldier, said to be an officer, did refuse, and fled away rather than carry out his orders. The name given is Robert Stewart. He does not appear in the muster roll of Glenlyon's company as recorded in October 1691; but there may have been some changes in the personnel since then, as the appearance of Lindsay and Lundie as Lieutenant and Ensign in place of Millon and Campbell proves. Robert Stewart is said to have gone off to the east side of the country and to have been protected by the Duke of Gordon who appointed him Forester of the Glenmore Forest in Strathspey. (*Scotland's Magazine*: May 1963.) As for the private soldiers, unless there had been changes there also, the two who may well have started the discontent (which led to some of them warning the inhabitants of their danger) were the two Mac-Eacherns, as they would have very distinct leanings towards Clan Donald. That name is common in Kintyre, and they were supporters of the Macdonalds of Islay. The Mac-Eacherns were both in Corporal Kennedy's No. 3 Section. Perhaps the presence of these two has been the foundation for the wild statements made by Campbells and others that the Massacre was carried out by Macdonalds against their own kin!

Although great secrecy was kept until the last possible moment in giving out the orders to the soldiers, some of them must have heard rumours even before the despatch came in that mysterious way in which news travels through an army. They seemed gloomy and depressed. During the day one of them was out in a field where some men were

working near Inverigan and was heard to address a great
stone in the field with the words "Ah! Great stone of the
Glen. If you knew what is to happen tonight, you would not
be lying so peaceful there!" The soldier seemed to wish the
men nearby to hear his words; and at any rate a small boy
did hear and reported them to Alasdair Òg and his wife. The
stone is still shown in a field on the left of the road as one
goes up towards Inverigan, but it is now much sunk into the
ground. It is known as MacEanruig's Stone from the name
of the boy who heard the soldier's words addressed to it. By
nine o'clock all the soldiers knew what was to be done. It
must not be supposed that any of them liked the business;
but from remarks let drop by some it is plain that they
regarded it as an order to be obeyed and the guilt, if any,
must lie with those who gave it—their superior officers.

By ten o'clock the Glen was asleep, except for the soldiers
and some restless souls who had reason for wakefulness. The
guards at the various posts had been doubled, thus with-
drawing as many as possible from among the houses of the
Macdonalds. The night was dark, and more snow was falling
developing into a blizzard with a bitter wind from the north.
Movement was thus difficult; but could be made secretly.
The vital points of Carnoch, Inverigan and Achnacon were
well covered by the doubled guards and others. These were
the places where the officers could see that the orders were
carried out. For the rest, there must have been many isolated
groups of houses which were under the guard of private
soldiers only, and it was here that without doubt some warning was given, directly or in some other way, to the indwellers to beware. Otherwise the Massacre would have
been much more successful and complete. It was at the places
where the officers were in control that the most corpses were
counted after the night of horror.

One who did not sleep that night was Alasdair Òg. He had
not been at all satisfied with Glenlyon's assurances when
asked why all the activity and doubling of guards. He went at
once to his brother, who treated the matter lightly. However,
they both went to MacIain's house and told him what was
going on. The old man too did not attach much importance
to Alasdair's apprehensions, and told them to go to bed,

adding that surely Glenlyon, after all his friendliness and even
accepting an invitation to dinner the following evening, could
be plotting no ill towards the people of the Glen. With that
they had to be content; but Alasdair went home with no
intention of resting. On their way home the brothers had to
pass one of the guardhouses and, creeping near, overheard
the soldiers awake and grousing, as soldiers will when called
out in the early hours. Amongst other remarks, the nature of
which one can easily guess, they heard one of them say to
another that he would not mind fighting the men of Glencoe
in battle, but this business did not seem to be the kind of duty
they should be asked to perform. The other replied that after
all they were only private soldiers and the blame would fall
on the officers who gave the orders. This confirmed the sus-
picions of the young MacIains, and one account says that
Alasdair at once ran to Inverigan and taxed Glenlyon with
duplicity, asking what all the stir was about unless some
hostile action was on foot. Glenlyon laughed at the idea,
repeated his excuses about the march to Glengarry, and
ended by asking him if he thought it possible that he could
be preparing any attack on his own niece, her husband and
their kin. No more was said and Alasdair had to leave; but
not feeling at all happy. Everything conspired to make him
more and more suspicious, and he kept awake. Meantime his
wife prepared for flight. She, even more than her husband,
was very suspicious and refused to rest, waiting for she knew
not what.

The hour fixed for the onslaught was five o'clock, and just
before that time a servant rushed into the house and told
Alasdair that soldiers were approaching with fixed bayonets.
He waited no longer. He and his wife fled, meeting his
brother on the way. Together they collected as many of their
people as they could and made for the slopes of Meall Mor.
On their way they narrowly escaped running into a party of
soldiers coming from the Ballachulish road, men of Duncanson's command; but they saw the soldiers before being themselves noticed, and avoided them. As they climbed along the
slopes of Meall Mor they heard the fusillades at Carnoch,
Inverigan and Achnacon. These same fusillades warned many
of the outlying hamlets before the soldiers allotted the task

of attacking them could get to the spot. It was a tactical error to use muskets, as from the time of the first shots the whole Glen was on the alert. Then, as the flames of the burning houses lit up the sky, the young men knew that their only course now was to gather as many of the survivors as possible and organize an escape.

Meantime MacIain and his wife were in bed when a knock came at the door. They replied and a servant asked who was there. A friendly voice which they recognized as Lindsay's answered that they had urgent business. The servant opened the door and Lindsay and the ensign rushed in and entered the bedroom. MacIain greeted them warmly; and, calling to the servant to serve drinks to their guests, he began to dress. His back was to the visitors as he pulled on his trews. Before he could turn round and face them, they both shot him—one through the back and the other through the head. He died instantly and fell by his bedside. Meantime his lady cried out and made to help her husband; but she was seized and treated in a shameful manner. Her rings were wrenched off, the assailants using their teeth to free them as they were very tightly held. Her clothes were stripped off her and she fled naked into the darkness. Somehow she managed to join a party of some of the refugees, but died of her injuries the following day. The servant was murdered, and an old man of eighty who was there. Another man, Duncan Donn, who came periodically to the Glen with letters was also shot and left for dead. The dead and dying were thrown on to the midden and left.

At Inverigan Glenlyon's men seized their host and eight men, bound them hand and foot and awaited their orders. Glenlyon gave the command and they were shot one after the other. It is here that an old story has its origin. When the nine men were seized, others including a woman and her baby, fled into the darkness. Soldiers were sent after them. After a long chase one of the soldiers came up with the woman and her babe hidden under a rock. As he approached, the soldier heard the woman crooning to her child a song he had heard his own wife singing to their own child, and could not bring himself to kill the unlucky pair. A dog had accompanied the woman in her flight, and the soldier killed it.

Dipping his sword in its blood he returned to Glenlyon to report that the deed had been done, showing the bloody blade in proof. The song sung by the woman is preserved in traditional form (see Appendix V).

At Achnacon Barbour was in charge. Eight men were sitting round the fire-side. Five o'clock seems a strange hour for such a meeting. Perhaps the general feeling of apprehension had spread. Achnacon himself sat there with Achtriochtan, the latter's brother and six more. On the stroke of five a volley of eighteen shots, fired through the windows by the sergeant and his men, laid six of them on the floor, dead or dying. Barbour came in and seeing one of them move asked him if he lived. Achtriochtan's brother was this man, according to the witnesses later examined at the Inquiry, and, when he replied that he was sorely wounded but still alive, Barbour made as if to finish him off. Macdonald begged that he be shot, if he had to be so murdered, outside the house; and Barbour magnanimously agreed, "seeing that he had eaten his meat for so many days". The victim was dragged out and propped up against the wall of the house. The morning being still dark, the firing party stood near to their quarry. Suddenly, Macdonald, who was a powerful man and not so badly wounded as he had made out, leapt forward, threw his plaid over the soldiers' muskets and escaped into the darkness with the shots of his would-be murderers falling harmlessly round and behind him. Meantime those not killed by the first volley had broken out of the back of the house and escaped. The descendants of this man live still in Scotland.

Down at Laroch the aged Ranald of the Targe, the hero of 1645, was shot and left for dead with his son. The latter was quite dead; but old Ranald managed to crawl to the shelter of a hut nearby. There, unable to move farther on account of his wounds, he perished in the flames when the hut and other farm-buildings were set on fire. He left two grandsons, who happened to be away from home. They survived and were "out" in 1745.

Glenlyon had hardly finished his fusillade of the nine unfortunate bound prisoners at Inverigan than Major Duncanson accompanied by Captain Drummond arrived to see how things had gone. They were not at all pleased. Neither had

any misgivings about their task. Drummond had already
shown his hate of MacIain by the incident at Barcaldine
where he had delayed the Chief for twenty-four precious hours
on his way to Inveraray. Duncanson was now to show his
ruthlessness. First he upbraided Glenlyon for his inefficiency
in not producing more corpses. Then he told him to get busy
and find some more. At this point a young man was found
still alive in the neighbourhood and dragged before the

Gable-end dated 1708 of the house of John Macdonald (son of the
murdered chief) at Invercoe. It was blown down in 1898. The
inscribed stone from this gable is now built into the gable of the
family vault on Eilean Munde. (From sketch by Noel Cook, lineal
descendant of the MacIains, from an old record.)

officers. Duncanson ordered Glenlyon to shoot him, and when
Campbell hesitated, Duncanson himself shot the prisoner. A
young boy of seven ran to Glenlyon and clasped him round
the knees begging for mercy. Drummond at once stabbed
the child through the back and he died at once. One more
body for the tally.

Duncanson's troops were those narrowly avoided by the
young MacIains after fleeing from their houses, and were
part of the company guarding the shore road to Appin. The
Major had left an officer in charge of the road block and had

come on to see if his help was needed in the mopping up operations. From the account of his meeting with Glenlyon it is plain that Campbell was tiring of the dreary business and not a little sickened by the Massacre already. The others had no such scruples; but only seemed angry that so few victims had been accounted for.

Meantime Hamilton with his company had been struggling

Stone from MacIain's house now set into the burial vault on Eilean Munde, with (above) "Burial Place of Macdonald of Glencoe" and (below it) "Stone from the ruined gable which fell 1898 of John Macdonald's house at Invercoe. He was eldest son of the massacred chief and was succeeded by his own eldest son, Alexr., who was attainted of high treason for joining the rising of 1715 and who was father of John Macdonald of Glencoe whose concern in the rising of 1745 led to the house being burned down and whose only son was Alexr. Macdonald of Glencoe. *ob.* 1814."

over the Staircase. The change in the weather, unforeseen when the operation was planned, hampered him badly. This old military road leaves Kinlochleven and winds round the shoulders of hills and through streams up to a summit of 1,850 feet, then for the last mile and a half drops steeply down the "staircase" to Alltnafeadh at the headwaters of the Etive River and a mile or so from the watershed at the east end of Glencoe. The distance is in all five and a half rough miles, difficult at the best of times, but, on a February morning in a blizzard, pretty fair hell. Hamilton arrived at last in the Glen below the watershed about nine o'clock and found no one there but one shepherd, an old man of eighty, one of Achtriochtan's men, whom he killed at once. The rest had fled long before and were making their way over the Lairig Eilde to Dalness. It was at this point that two officers refused to go on with the business, sickened by the murder of the octogenarian. These were Lieutenants Francis Farquhar and Gilbert Kennedy. They were immediately put under close arrest, and later sent to Glasgow. They gave evidence at the Inquiry; and it is not likely that any drastic disciplinary action was taken in view of the popular outcry against the murders.

Finding no corpses on his way down the Glen, by the time he met the disconsolate group of officers at Inverigan, Hamilton was furious and was in no mood to listen to Glenlyon's excuses. He too poured scorn on the Captain's achievements. While they were thus arguing a soldier came up and gave them some papers he had found on two of the bodies, Achtriochtan's and another's, which proved to be the letters from Hill jealously guarded by the two unfortunates in the belief that in them they had protection. The letters were at once destroyed. Such evidence was best out of the way. All that remained now was to scour the ruins of the hamlets for any survivors, burn the few houses that were left and gather the stock for removal to Inverlochy. A few corpses were found, one of a woman, and a baby's hand. The private soldiers, left to themselves, had not done very well. Their warnings had not fallen on deaf ears. It is hard to say if the playing of the pibroch ever took place, and if so at what point in the proceedings it could have done any good. If the piper had played without orders before the appointed time he would surely have been punished and the fact recorded. If after the killing had begun, then it would have been just a little too late to be of use to the Macdonalds, except those nearby. It seems much more likely that it was played later when the curtain had fallen, and the officers and men needed cheering up. "Breadalbane's March" has now words set to it far different from those used at Allt nam Meirleach. (See Appendix VI.)

Stories handed down to this day hold that some of the Campbell soldiers were killed in the "fray". It is hard to believe that some bold spirit did not seize a dirk out of the thatch and attack his assailants. One place was pointed out to the writer as the grave of a Campbell. It is in the angle of the deer-fence which runs at right-angles to the old road up the slopes of the Pap, between Bridge of Coe and Leac an Tuim. There may be other places; but the fact remains that no casualties are reported in the official inquiry; and surely they would have been if in fact they had taken place. It would have been very difficult for any Macdonald to get quickly at his arms, which, as soon as Glenlyon's company approached the Glen, had been hidden in very safe places. Much as a Macdonald might wish that one at least of the enemy had died, it must be assumed that no such incident took place.

When everything possible had been done, and the corpses counted, it was found that in all 38 persons had been killed. The rest, the great majority, had vanished. The stock was collected to the number of 900 head of cattle, 200 horses, and a great number of sheep and goats, and got ready for their departure.

So ended the Massacre of Glencoe. The plan had been carried out "secretly and suddenly", but not quite entirely as planned. Several avenues of escape had been left unguarded after all, and the little clan was not annihilated. From the grandiose scheme of wiping out the Clans Cameron, Glengarry, Keppoch, Stewart, Maclean and Glencoe, the conspirators had been forced to descend to the destruction of the smallest of these, and even that had been bungled. They had incurred the ignominy, guilt and execration without achieving the object of the exercise.

Of all the atrocities committed that morning the murder of the Chief epitomizes them all. Old MacIain, under whose orders the people of the Glen had extended hospitality to some sixty to one hundred visitors, was, in the very act of ordering drinks for his guests at an unprecedented hour of the morning, struck down by those very guests—brutally through the back. They did not even give him the satisfaction of one last look of scorn as he fell. This is the deed which so shocked the world at the time, and has done so ever since. And yet it was not done by the hand of his hereditary foes but by two Scots (Lowlanders it is true), not even Englishmen, under orders from their Campbell commander. And those who cause others to commit a crime have to bear the responsibility.

Chapter Nine

ESCAPE AND RETURN

By noon the slaughter was over and thirty-eight corpses lay on the middens and dung-heaps round the clachans—the last indignity imposed on the hated little clan. The valley was empty except for the soldiers searching the rubble for loot, and others collecting the stock preparatory to the march to Inverlochy. None of the Macdonalds were left alive in the habitable lower reaches of the Glen. There was nothing to keep the soldiers now. The hospitable hearths round which they had passed the long evenings for the last fortnight were now smouldering heaps of thatch and rubble. The victorious company formed up, Glenlyon at its head with Lindsay and the ensign, and Sergeant Barbour bringing up the rear. Drummers Dalzell and Hunter headed the procession; and, although no mention is made of a piper in the muster-rolls, Glenlyon may have had a private piper, as befitted a petty chieftain. It is not likely that a piper could compose a pibroch for such an occasion, nor that any of that dishonoured company felt in the mood for music, as they marched out of the smoking valley, leaving it to the buzzards and ravens.

From the time that the first shot was fired at five o'clock the people began to scatter. It was a tactical error to use muskets as the noise advertised in no uncertain manner what was going on. The fugitives made off in all directions to the hills and rocks, wherever they could find temporary shelter from the murderers. In this flight many of the weaker fell never to rise again. Others, hidden in caves and crevices of the rocks, died miserably of exposure. The numbers who died thus have been variously estimated; but certainly they could have been no less than those who perished at the hands of the soldiers. It is impossible to be sure; but we do know that many survived, otherwise how could MacIain have led close on a hundred fighting men out to Sheriffmuir twenty-three years later? What happened? What avenues of escape were open to the weaker members of the clan—the aged, the women and children?

Northwards all escape for such was hopeless. Duncanson was a very efficient soldier and had his patrols out along the shores of the Loch. Hamilton similarly had his pickets at the head of the Loch. The continuous wall of splintered rock which runs from the sea over the Pap, Sgorr nam Fiannaidh, and Aonach Eagach for eight jagged and perilous miles to the Staircase quite shut them in. Moreover the boats had all been secured under guard. Even so tradition states that a few active young men made good their escape to Mamore and even as far as the bounds of Keppoch's country. That was, however, no solution to the problem for the majority. Their minds turned at once to the only two possible places where they could be safe—Dalness and Appin. The first belonged to their own kinsfolk. Alasdair of Dalness and his people had been left out of the plans for extermination, perhaps because they were tenants of Campbell of Inverawe, or because to net both glens—Glencoe and Glen Etive—was well-nigh impossible. That then was one sanctuary: the other was among the friendly Stewarts of Appin. The next problem was how to get there. They must have reviewed in their minds all the possible passes leading out of their trap. There are several.

In examining these we must remember all the time that the pathetic bands of fugitives were made up of all sorts of folk—old men and women, children, women with babes at the breast, and pregnant women. Some way had to be found that was feasible for weaker ones to travel and yet be out of sight of the soldiers before daylight came.

The exit of the Glen south-eastwards led only to the Moor of Rannoch and meant a journey of many miles ending up in the wastes of that dreary wilderness.

This, even leaving out of account Hamilton's troops entering the Glen from the Staircase, was obviously hopeless. As one comes down the Glen from Rannoch Moor the first pass leading south is the Lairig Gartain which opens directly opposite Alltnafeadh at the bottom of the Staircase.

From Achnacon it is more than six miles to the pass, and from Carnoch eight. Thereafter four more miles have to be covered over the pass to Dalness. Considering that the refugees would have had to avoid the easier tracks and keep up on the slopes of the mountains in case they met patrols of the enemy, it would seem impossible that any made good their escape that way.

The next opening in the hills, about two miles down the Glen from the Lairig Gartain, is the Lairig Eilde (The Pass of the Hind), a shorter route to Dalness, although a little higher to climb. This was the best way for the remnants of Achtriochtan's tenants to take; and it was the last straggler of this party who was caught by Hamilton's men on their way down the Glen and killed. He was eighty years of age and could not make enough speed to reach the pass before he was caught, or perhaps he preferred to risk it and stay at home. Either way the poor old man had no chance of survival.

Leaving the Lairig Eilde there is no break in the mountains until we come to the Lairig Fhionnghaill, a long and high pass into Glen Etive leading to the hamlet of Invercarnan, below Dalness. This may have been used by some; but to get into it they would have to cross the mouth of Gleann Muidhe near Achnacon, a wide stretch of open country, on which they had little cover.

The last outlet from the main glen leaves the bend in the river at Achnacon and runs up into the hills south-east— Gleann Muidhe, where MacIain had his farm, and quite a few of his people lived.

This was the most attractive of all the outlets. It led in the right direction, by the shortest route, to the sanctuary of Appin. It is here that tradition states the majority of the survivors made their escape. The glen runs for over a mile into the hills and then forks. From that point it is possible to turn north into the Laroch Glen, go on into Glen Creran, or by climbing another short pass reach Glen Duror in the heart of the Stewart country. From Carnoch to the watershed between Glen Muidhe and Glen Creran is five miles, not an impossible task for any able to walk at all. Travelling at a mile an hour the weaker members could be at the summit before full daylight could reveal them to their pursuers.

All these passes should have been secured by the Campbell clansmen of Argyll and Breadalbane according to the orders; but for some reason they seem to have been neglected. Perhaps the Campbells preferred to wait for their prey farther south beyond the Moor of Rannoch, leaving the garrisons at Barcaldine and Castle Stalker to watch Etive and Appin. Whatever the reason, these passes were open, and that saved the remnants of Clann Iain from extinction.

John MacIain, now Chief of the Clan, and his brother had, as we have seen, gathered as many of the survivors as they could, after eluding Duncanson's men. As they skirted the slopes of Meal Mor well above the floor of the Glen they could see the fires started in the houses and hear the shots of the killers. Their shortest route from there to safety would plainly be to follow the contours round the shoulder of Meall Mor into Glen Muidhe and keep going up to the head of that glen. On their way they were joined by fugitives from Inverigan and Achnacon. On the southern slopes of the hill in Gleann Muidhe they were sheltered to some extent from the north wind and snow showers, and yet kept out of sight (at this early hour) of the soldiers below.

This, the only organized party, contained some hundred and twenty souls. Men and women, young and old, children— all were represented. Young MacIain led them on encouraging the weak and keeping them going as best he could. It was essential to be out of the Glen before day broke. A nurse carried in her arms his own son, a baby, and this child lived to become in his turn Chief of the Clan. Amongst them was a grandfather, Ewan, carrying in his arms his grandchild, Ewan Òg. The mother had been killed with her husband and the old grandfather alone was left to save the baby, whose descendants live now in Canada. There were many cases such as this; and it was a sadly depleted and exhausted convoy that followed the young Chief into Appin. Some had fallen by the way, but most of them got through—the nucleus of the new Clann Iain which rose out of the ashes under the kindly care of the Appin Stewarts.

For the rest, isolated groups of two or three made their way through the other passes to Dalness, thence, after resting, to join the main body in Appin. It is impossible to

Alasdair Òg, second son of the murdered Chief, who escaped from the Massacre in 1692. He married Elspeth, daughter of Stewart of Ardsheal, and as his second wife, in 1692, Florence Macdonald. He died in 1707.

Robert Campbell of Glenlyon, captain in Argyll's Regiment in 1692.
He died, a colonel, in Flanders in 1696 (*photo:* National Galleries of
Scotland).

guess how many died of exposure on their way to safety. In many Macdonald families the story is still told how their ancestors were fugitives from the Massacre who went far from their native valley and settled in distant 'parts of the country—Moray, Aberdeen and Perthshire—never to return. It is quite understandable that many who had seen their near relatives murdered before their eyes might not wish ever to see Glencoe again.

Before very long, once all the soldiers had been withdrawn, the survivors began to come back in small groups to bury the dead.

Little by little the bolder members of the clan came back to their native valley and began to build up the houses and make ready for a full return of their families. It was not till later that official sanction was given. Meantime, not long after the disaster, Campbell of Barcaldine, as agent for Breadalbane, came to the two young MacIains and proposed that they should certify that Breadalbane had had nothing to do with the affair in any way; and in return they were offered "full restitution". How the Earl could undertake this on behalf of the Government does not appear; but it just shows that one of the conspirators was feeling uneasy, although no word had yet come through that there would be any official inquiry at all.

When the news leaked out wild rumours were current in Edinburgh first and London later. Some of these were very far from the truth. One reported that a clan battle had been fought; that the Campbells had made a night attack which had resulted in the complete extermination of the Macdonalds. The neighbouring clans in Lochaber who knew the truth were aghast and made ready for their own defence, naturally expecting that it would be their turn next to suffer the pacifying influences of the King and his servants. The Jacobites at once made capital of the reports and rumours; and the King became very unpopular, so much so that one historian thought that, if James had landed at that time with any force, William might have been expelled. This is an exaggeration; but there is no doubt but that the stock of the Government fell very low; and when the real facts came to light later matters were not improved.

Hill was the man on the spot, and his letters of this period are very enlightening. In these he does not seem to be the genial friend of the clans one might have thought before the Massacre took place. The following are extracts from some of his letters to Tweeddale, Lord Chancellor, at this time.

On 4th February, before the Massacre, he wrote that Glengarry had come in and taken the oath "according to an order he had to the effect". This must refer to the special clause in the King's Order empowering him to treat with Glengarry in any way he thought fit so long as the castle of Invergarry was secured and he took the oath, even after due date. On the 14th, Hill wrote again "Invergarry surrendered Thursday last. Party sent to Island Donan with strict order from Buchan to garrison to hand it over, which I believe is done ere this if the horrid storm on Friday does not retard him. I have also ruined Glencoe. Old Glencoe and Achtriaton (the two chiefs of the two families of the Clanean in Glencoe) being killed with thirty-six more, the rest by reason of an extraordinary storm escaped, but their goods are a prey and their houses to the fire, who may get other broken men to join them and be very troublesome to the country of which (not to trouble your Lordship) I have written more fully to the Commander in Chief and about a proclamation which will be necessary to be issued out against them. They come from all parts to submit to the King's mercy and to take the oath of allegiance and (according to my orders) save their lives. I hope this example of justice and severity upon Glencoe will be enough."

There is no remorse apparent in these letters, nor is the later letter, written in March, in which he seeks to justify himself, any better. On the 17th he sent a full account of the destruction of Glencoe to Tweeddale by the hand of Captain Cunningham of his own regiment.

The rumours flying round Edinburgh were now coming back to Lochaber, much exaggerated, if that were possible, in a way rumours have if left to circulate long enough. Hill began to get a little apprehensive, and wrote once more to Tweeddale (he was a great letter-writer, for which the historian may be thankful) amongst others, on 28th March:

"If these poor people that remain of the Glencoe men may be accepted to mercy and pardon, taking the oath and giving security for their future peaceable living, it might be well what is done being enough for example and vindication of the public justice. I make no doubt but to keep them civil and in good order they will always, as many others do, fear such another stroak." And again: "I understand that there are some severe reflections upon the action in Glencoe, and that perhaps by many good men too. Therefore I think it my duty to give your Lordship a more particular account thereof. Glencoe came to me and I advised him to haste to the Sheriff and take the oath before the day, which he promised to do, and I would not let him stay so much as to drink but he turned about and went to Glengarry and let the time elapse, but wrote to the Sheriff three days after and what he did then was not sustained because after the day. Upon which I had several orders from the Commander in Chief and all extraordinary strict to destroy these people and take no prisoners, and (lest I should prove remiss) another of the same orders was directed to my Lieutenant-Colonel to do the same, and after all that another order under the King's own hand to root out that sept of thieves, but by the help of a storm several of the men escaped who yet are quiet in hopes they may obtain a pardon for their lives upon giving security for their peaceable living which in my humble opinion were better than to turn them desperate and to join with other loose men and lie in every bush and glen in small parties to shoot men and rob up and down the country as they find their fittest occasions, and I doubt not but I could make them peaceable. If any censure the severity of man's justice, yet the Justice of God is to be reverenced for there was much blood on these people's hands, and either these orders must be disobeyed (that were hard pressed by authority) or else these people must have suffered what they had done."

The question arises how MacIain was able to visit Glengarry after leaving Hill that day. The Chief of Glengarry may well have been in the vicinity at the time, which would mean that to see him meant little delay in MacIain's movements. It must have been quite impossible for him to go to Invergarry and yet return in time to arrive in Inveraray even by the 6th January, which he undoubtedly did. It rather looks as if Hill wished to present MacIain's actions in a bad light, in order to detract from the guilt of the murders.

In April the affair was still being talked of in Edinburgh and now the first printed report of it appeared on the 12th in the Paris *Gazette*. This version was accurate except that it included the statement that MacIain's two sons had died with their father. This caused alarm in London and we have the first written report issued in England in the form of a letter from a gentleman in Edinburgh to his friend in London who had asked for the truth. (See Appendix VII.) At first this letter was assumed to be one of the exaggerated rumours already put out by the Jacobites; but, as time went on, and the truth began to emerge, more and more credence was given to it, and the public conscience began to wake up. By summer both capitals knew the truth. Argyll's Regiment had been withdrawn from the Highlands shortly after the Massacre, and was by this time in Brentford awaiting orders to embark for Flanders. On 30th June a Jacobite gentleman visited Brentford and saw both Glenlyon and Drummond. He also talked to some of the soldiers concerned in the affair, and they confirmed the truth of the news now current that the Glencoe men had been "slaughtered under trust", which was of course the factor which enraged folk much more than the bare fact of the killing. "Under trust" were the operative words, which appeared later in the official inquiry of 1695. Glenlyon was now living in a continual state of nerves, and one could "see Glencoe in his face". In Edinburgh when the regiment was on its way south, he had been quite confident; and in the taverns he had been heard stoutly to assert that what he had done he would do again if ordered to do so, as befitted a faithful soldier of His Majesty. By the time he got to Brentford his conscience had begun to work.

On the 3rd May the first official move to reinstate the MacIains was made. They were given protection by the Privy Council, which did not restore their lands and goods, but at least they could feel safe from any such base attack in the future. As to the re-settlement of the clan in their own glen, some were of the opinion that any but Macdonalds should be installed in those lands. Hill did not receive this order from the Council until the 21st of May; but reported from time to time that the Glencoe men were very quiet, and he had no fears about making them peaceful, while at the same time giving a warning in no uncertain terms that a full settlement was urgent if they were not to be drawn to desperation. He pointed out that if they continued in a state of outlawry, other broken men would join them, and a band of four hundred might easily collect to carry on a guerilla warfare which would be difficult to put down. This state of affairs dragged on until June, and the MacIains still waited for the "King's mercy to settle them back in their own country". They were living where they could, among hospitable neighbours in Appin and Lochaber, while some had already made a start on their own farms, although quite without the sanction of the Government. They showed every sign of wishing to live in peace, and yet in July Hill was still asking for a decision, as they were nearly starving.

At last, in August, the King gave in to Hill's importunity and sanctioned their return to the Glen under the protection of Hill, who was to answer for their good behaviour. So at last the little clan was back home again, trying to make some of the houses habitable and gather enough food for the on-coming winter. Many friends helped them in this task: Keppoch, Locheil and the Stewarts of Appin. Food came from a distance too. One notable case is on record. Far out in the Western ocean the laird of Heiskir, an island some miles to the west of North Uist, Alasdair Bàn Mac Iain 'Ic Uisdein (to give him his Gaelic patronymic) loaded his birlinn with meal and sailed through the dangerous seas of the Minch and up Loch Linnhe to the shores of Loch Leven at the mouth of Glencoe, where his grateful kinsfolk un-loaded the welcome cargo. It is not to be supposed that he was the only member of Clan Donald to do such an act of kindness, but he must have been the most distant in time and space. Alexander of Heiskir was a cadet of the House of Sleat, one of the Clann Dómhnaill Hearaich; so the ancestor common to himself and MacIain of Glencoe lived away back in 1300. Such ties, considered very distant in these days, were held very strongly among the Gaels, whose sense of kinship and genealogy, has always been highly developed. Heiskir, and indeed the whole of Clan Donald, regarded themselves as near cousins of the unfortunate Clann Iain.

The winter passed quietly, and not much is on record to show how things went in Glencoe; but the clan survived somehow. In October Hill had tried to have them placed under the "protection" of Argyll, as he deemed it necessary "they should be under some person of power and honesty to the Government". A sad and ironic turn of Fate that they should have to rely on the biggest Campbell of all for "protection!" Stewart of Appin, under whom they had been at one time, was not much better off. Argyll protected him too.

At last, in March of 1693 the Scots Parliament met after a recess of two and a half years. The Duke of Hamilton was Lord High Commissioner, and Stair and Johnstone joint Secretaries. Stair was in Flanders with the King, so Johnstone acted at home. In a session of two months little mention was made of Glencoe in spite of all the popular interest in it. A law was passed giving special powers to Argyll against the Highlanders.

Public opinion and the repeated demands that an inquiry should be held became so urgent now that the King at last set up a Committee of Inquiry to look into the matter. The Duke of Hamilton was in charge with orders to inquire into the slaughter and the manner in which it had been carried out. The Duke died on the 27th April, so he must have been a sick man at the time of his appointment. Anyway the results of this inquiry were deemed "defective". No one was satisfied with it, and it was soon forgotten. All it did was to make the guilty men begin to think, and wonder what they were to say if called on as witnesses. Livingstone wrote to Lt.-Colonel Hamilton that there was an agitation starting, and hinted that it might be as well to give it some thought. They had two full years to make up their minds how they should explain their actions because the next, and final, inquiry was not instituted until 1695. At this time, the King was much more occupied with the affairs of his wars abroad, and the wrangling of the churchmen at home. None of them seemed to be satisfied. We have seen that Stair was not very zealous in any direction as far as religion was concerned. All he wanted was a settlement of some kind so long as the Government was left in peace. In order to see where the churchmen stood the King demanded that all, Presbyterians and Episcopalians alike, should take an oath of allegiance similar to that exacted from the chiefs. Here he met more opposition than he expected. The Presbyterians refused as they regarded William to be little better than an Erastian or Laodicean, while the Episcopalians denied that he was the lawful King anyway. Their combined operation was so great that, on the advice of Carstairs who kept him right on matters spiritual, William did not press it, and the matter was dropped.

Nothing more is heard of Glencoe, apart from the usual rumours, until 1695, three full years after the event, when the matter could be ignored no longer. The King wisely saw that he would have to do something; and, rather than be compelled to act under pressure, he appointed a Royal Commission with full powers to inquire into the whole business, call witnesses and report their findings to him and Parliament. At long last there seemed to be a ray of hope. Perhaps justice was about to be done.

Chapter Ten

INQUIRY AND VERDICT

THE Royal Commission was appointed at Kensington the 29th April 1695 and sealed and registered in Edinburgh on the 20th May. The Marquis of Tweeddale, Lord High Chancellor, was at its head, with the Earl of Annandale and seven others under him. The composition of this body was impressive, being made up of the most important legal officers of the Government. It will be noted that the Lord Advocate was Sir James Steuart, who took the place when, according to the letter quoted already (see Appendix VII), Sir John Lowther refused the office unless he were permitted to institute an inquiry into Glencoe. Annandale took the leading part in calling witnesses and conducting the business of the inquiry. He called as many witnesses as he could find. Hill was summoned to come himself and bring seven or eight of the officers or men, who were present at the Massacre, for questioning (see Appendix VIII). The witnesses mentioned in the report include the two sons of MacIain: two Macdonalds (Archibald and Ranald): Ardkinglas, Sheriff of Argyll: Colin Campbell, Sheriff Clerk of Argyll: Lord Aberuchil: John Campbell, W.S.: Sir Gilbert Elliot: David Moncreiff, Clerk of the Council: James Campbell, a private soldier of Argyll's Regiment who had not gone to Flanders with it, but had been in Glencoe's company at the Massacre: Major John Forbes: Sir Thomas Livingstone: and Lt.-Colonel James Hamilton. All these attended except the last who thought it safer to absent himself, and sent a letter of apology to Annandale (see Appendix IX).

The Commission started work at once and carried out their duties well and expeditiously. Their appointment was dated the 20th May (see Appendix X) and they produced their findings on the 20th June. The Report is very full and covers much of the matter already narrated in previous chapters so it is only necessary here to extract the important parts, leaving the reader to consult for himself the full draft (see Appendix XI).

The headings under which they conducted their business were four: (1) the matters which preceded the Massacre: (2) the matter of fact with proofs and evidence taken, when and in what manner the slaughter was committed: (3) the warrants and directions that either really were, or were claimed, for the committing of it: (4) the Commissioners' opinion of the truth of the matter. They went carefully through all the evidence and found (1) that the obliteration of the oath taken by MacIain was wrong, as it was done without the warrant of the Council in full session: (2) that the Master of Stair did know that MacIain had taken the oath, even though it was taken after due date: (3) that nothing in King William's instructions warranted the slaughter, even the thing itself, far less the manner in which it was carried out: (4) that Stair's letters were the only warrant for the crime of "slaughter under trust". In support of the last finding, Stair's letters written afterwards were quoted. On the 5th March he wrote to Hill that he regretted that any of the Macdonalds had escaped. In April he told Hill not to worry, "when you are right, fear no one . . . but in the execution it was neither so full nor so fair as might have been". The general verdict was that it was a barbarous murder perpetrated by the "persons deponed against".

Parliament received the report on the 24th June, and voted *nem. con.* that His Majesty's instructions of the 11th and 16th January 1692 . . . did "contain a warrant for mercy to all, without exception, who should take the oath of allegiance, and come in upon mercy, though the first day of January 1692, prefixed by the proclamation of indemnity, was passed: and that therefore these instructions contained no warrant for the execution of the Glenco-men in February thereafter". It was then voted that the execution of the Glenco-men, as represented to Parliament, was a murder. The method of prosecution of the guilty was delayed till the following Monday. On the 26th Parliament considered Stair's letters and decided that they exceeded the King's Commission, towards the killing and destroying of the Glenco-men. On the 28th notice was taken of a pamphlet which had been circulated to all Members of Parliament entitled "Information for the Master of Stair". This paper stated that Stair had "been mightily prejudged by the Report of the Commission, which notices particular sentences or periods of certain letters, and from whence consequences were drawn which cannot follow upon a due consideration of the whole". The author was found to be Hew Dalrymple, younger brother of the Master of Stair. The paper was declared to be false and calumnious, an apology demanded, and the paper condemned to be burned.

Then they decided that Sir Thomas Livingstone had every reason to pass on the orders he had received from the King. On 8th July Parliament resumed sitting and considered the case of Lt.-Colonel Hamilton and decided there was ground for prosecuting him. Duncanson came under the same condemnation and it was recommended that he should be called home from Flanders to be prosecuted, "as His Majesty shall think fit". They went on with the other cases and decided that Glenlyon, Drummond, Lt. Lindsay, Ensign Lundie, and Sergeant Barbour should be brought home and tried for the "murder of the Glenco-men under trust". On 10th July Parliament sent their findings in the form of an Address to the King (see Appendix XII) with several of Stair's letters to Livingstone and Hill. There was some debate as to whether they should include the paragraph about Stair or not; but it was voted to include it.

It is patent, reading these two documents, the Report and the Address, that the efforts of the Scots lords and lawyers were bent on exonerating the King and casting the whole blame on Stair.

In the midst of all these reports and letters, so detailed and so full, where is one to find the truly guilty man, or men? The long list of accused persons falls into two main categories: the Government, which includes the King, his Secretary Stair, the Privy Council in Edinburgh, the Sheriff of Argyll and his Clerk: secondly, the Army, which includes all from the Commander-in-Chief, Livingstone, down to the last private soldier in Glenlyon's and Hamilton's companies. The fact is that all of these, in both categories, except for the Sheriff of Argyll and his Clerk, are guilty in varying degrees.

King William was guilty because he signed the order which led to the Massacre. It is little use saying that he did not know what he was signing, that he signed it among many other state papers and so it escaped his eye, or that he trusted his Secretary to put the right kind of order in front of him. He ought to have read a document affecting the lives and fortunes of so many of his subjects, even if they were a remote tribe on the outskirts of his dominions. The double signature, above and below, has nothing to do with it, except that it prevented Stair's signature appearing on the paper, as it might have done had the King superscribed only. It has been said that this was an evil design of Stair's to avert blame from himself and throw it all on the King. Whether this is true or not matters little as there are other documents and letters signed by Stair sufficient to condemn him. He is the one man of all the Government employees who must carry the blame for the Massacre. It was his rancour and hate which urged on the others to carry out their treacherous work. He murdered the victims of the Massacre as surely as if he had done it with his own hands.

Excuse is often made for the planners and executors of the slaughter to justify their action by saying that the Macdonalds of Glencoe were thieves and murderers. We have shown that much of their livelihood depended upon cattle-lifting (to use the term usually applied to that form of military operation); and it has been admitted that this was the case; but, although cattle were lifted, few lives were lost in the process, and none were killed treacherously. On the other hand, if the King and Stair wished to root out any of their subjects guilty of the unfair acquisiton of the property of others, they should in all equity have started with Breadalbane and Argyll, whose activities were much more far-reaching than the mere appropriation of a few cows. Their technique, already referred to, of "harrying their less powerful neighbours", and gaining superiority over their lives and property, was surely no less disturbing to the peace of the realm?

The Privy Council, or at least those members who received the letters and certified oath from Ardkinglas, are guilty for not proroguing the execution until the King's mind was sought on the matter and he given a chance to show mercy, even although his orders expressly excluded Glencoe. They had the original order to consult in which it was plain that William was willing to extend the date in certain cases, notably that of Glengarry. The Council in full session might well have given a very different opinion to that pronounced by the few members who dealt with the Sheriff's urgent appeal for consideration. In spite of his request that he be informed of the action taken, it seems that he did not hear of the obliteration of MacIain's oath until too late to do anything. His powers were not great as Sheriff of Argyll; but judging by his behaviour towards MacIain it is very unlikely that he would have been party to the cancellation. Ardkinglas and his Clerk must be judged clear of blame. They both did their best to help MacIain and avoid the slaughter.

So much for the Government: the blame lies equally on the King and Stair, and on the members of the Privy Council, who dealt with the matter, to a much lesser degree. Although the Report throws much blame on them, in fairness one has to give them the benefit of some doubt. After all they acted strictly according to law and directions from above.

As for the Army commanders and soldiers: they were, of course, soldiers under orders from the political powers, and might claim that it was their duty to carry out orders given them by the Government, no matter what those orders were. This excuse was given at the War Criminals' trials after the late War; but did not absolve Keitel and other soldiers from sentence of death. Taking the list of all those concerned from the top down: Livingstone, Hill, Hamilton, Duncanson, Drummond, Glenlyon, Lindsay, Lundie, Barbour and the private soldiers—all are to blame in an increasing degree as one descends in the scale, although not all the private soldiers are to be included in this condemnation. Some at least held their hands from blood, and others went out of their way to warn their intended victims.

Livingstone received and transmitted his orders without embellishing them. As far as he was concerned it was just another raid on hostile tribes and he left the details of its execution to his subordinates. Hill is a special case. He is not free from blame, in spite of his actions in trying to help MacIain by his letter to Ardkinglas. He is rather to be judged by his reactions after, and his apparent satisfaction at having "ruined Glencoe" followed by his cold-blooded report that MacIain and thirty-nine more had been butchered. He was not, after all, the genial character we were inclined to believe him before the event. His blame is much the same as Livingstone's—in being a link in the chain of orders which led inevitably to the Massacre.

Duncanson, Drummond and Hamilton can be taken together, as they, of all the soldiers concerned, showed extreme brutality, not minding how the killing was carried out so long as the tally of corpses was satisfactorily lengthy. They too planned in detail the "netting" of the Glen, and it was not their fault that any escaped. To the bitter end they tried their hardest to add to the list, not sparing even little boys and very old men.

Glenlyon, Lindsay, Lundie and Barbour are the worst of all that grisly band. They were the ones who lived in the Glen for a fortnight before the attack, and so basely betrayed the trust put in them by their hosts.

Glenlyon is the name irrevocably linked with the Massacre. There are some extenuating circumstances in his case; and we must in fairness examine all these before condemning him out of hand. He was a Campbell and therefore disliked, to say the least, all Macdonalds. He had suffered from the predatory instincts of the MacIains in the raid of 1689 to such an extent that he had been obliged to take up employment in the Army, a thing he was not too keen on doing, but was forced to in order to keep himself and his family alive. His character was complex. Even his kinsman, Breadalbane, had doubts as to his mental stability, as the letter of that gentleman to his agent, Campbell of Carwhin, shows. In January 1690 Breadalbane wrote: "Glenlyon ought to be sent to Bedlam as he, Duncan, used his great-grandfather. I wish I had chambered him some years ago." There follows an account of Glenlyon having raised a number of men in Argyll and led them plundering in Glenorchy and Strathfillan until challenged by the local lairds. Breadalbane goes on, "He is an object of compassion when I see him, but when he is out of my sight I could wish he had never been born!"

Perhaps there is ground for suspecting Glenlyon of some mental instability if Breadalbane is to be believed; and one might put in a plea of "diminished responsibility" in accordance with modern usage. But when all has been said in his defence, his guilt remains as black as ever. On this side of the balance we have the flagrant abuse of the sacred laws of hospitality as understood by the Gael; and he was a Gael and should have known better. That is the ingredient that sours the whole dismal business. "Slaughter under trust" are the words used by the Commission to describe the crime which has made the name of Glenlyon notorious ever since. One can remember with pleasure the very different behaviour of another Campbell towards this traditional law of hospitality sixty-six years later—Major Duncan Campbell of Inverawe who fell at Ticonderoga in 1758. (See Appendix XIV). To live with a family for a fortnight under the most friendly circumstances, to accept an invitation to dinner with that family, and then on the same day to order the murder of the head of that family, is surely the basest form of crime that could ever be imagined. That was bad enough; but after all Glenlyon was not himself present at the murder of the old Chief and his Lady, even if it was he who did it, as surely as if his hand had held the pistol and fired it into the back of MacIain's head—from the back. Much worse was the tying up of nine helpless prisoners and then having them shot one by one in front of his eyes, one of them being his own host of the past two weeks. This last atrocity seems to have sickened him, and he took no further active part in the killing; but that was just a little too late to avoid the stigma of slaughter under trust. His boasts in the Edinburgh taverns afterwards, in vino, do not seem to indicate any remorse or change of heart, whatever he may have suffered later.

Lindsay and Lundie were worse than their Captain. Their orders were to deal with MacIain—orders which they carried out in the most brutal manner, and then they seem to have gone mad; for to strip an elderly lady of all her clothes and tear off her rings, driving her out into the night, was beyond the command to kill the males between seven and seventy.

The military orders founded on the King's own commands changed as they were transmitted down the line. They become progressively more virulent: the element of treachery creeps in: and we have to lay the blame for that on Hamilton and Duncanson. They devised the surrounding of the folk of the Glen by a pincer movement—their two companies being the jaws of the pincer. It is not quite clear whose bright idea it was to have Glenlyon's company in the heart of the Glen for so long before the event to lull the Macdonalds into a sense of security. It may well have been the child of Breadalbane's fertile brain; but, if it was, he made sure that it did not come out at the inquiry.

We come now to that noble earl and his part in all this. He was in a way between the Government and the Army, belonging to neither officially, advising both with his special knowledge, and unobtrusively encouraging them in their designs. His character was so tortuous that it is impossible to prove his part in it. We do know he was in London and in close touch with Argyll and Stair during those vital days before the Massacre. The three dined together at times, and must have discussed the whole plot over and over again. The two Campbells in that party kept their names clear of official accusation, while Dalrymple did the writing, unfortunately for him. Breadalbane's character is succinctly summed up by Macaulay in his *History of England*, thus: "He seems to have united two different sets of vices, the growth of two different regions and of two different stages in the progress of society. In his castle away in the hills he had learned the barbarous pride and ferocity of a Highland chief. In the Council chamber of Edinburgh he had contracted the deep taint of treachery and corruption. After the Revolution he had, like many of his fellow nobles, betrayed every party in turn, had sworn fealty to William and Mary, and had plotted against them. To trace all the turns and doublings of his course would be wearisome." As we have seen he managed to avoid any trouble for the private articles of the Achachallader meeting by telling the Government he had undertaken to raise 1,000 men of his clan for any future rising in favour of

King James so that he might be in the chiefs' confidence and
be able to betray their councils. Stair believed him; and he
escaped. One who could evade that danger was well able to
keep his designs and actions secret, so no one managed to
bring him to book for any part in the Massacre. He is mentioned twice only in the Report—once in connection with the
meeting at Achachallader when the Glenco-men witnessed
that he had threatened to do MacIain a damage for his attitude at that meeting, by which the whole business was
wrecked. The second mention is when he approached, through
the mediation of his agent, Barcaldine, the two sons of
MacIain, promising them restitution if they denied that he
had had any part in the plans for the Massacre. It is not
apparent how he had the power to promise such restitution.
Perhaps it was only an undertaking to use his good offices
with the powers in trying to get their application considered. It did show, however, that he had something on his
mind, if not on his conscience.

The name of Argyll does not appear in either the Report of
the Royal Commission or in the Address to the King, except
that he told Stair that Glencoe had not come in to take the
oath in time, and it was his regiment which took part in the
Massacre. In themselves these references do not incriminate
Argyll himself. The other records mention him only in
Stair's report that he and Breadalbane would secure the
southern passes so that none should escape by those routes.
In fact Argyll did not do his part in that manœuvre, for some
reason which it would be hard to prove now, and yet it was
precisely through those passes that the majority of the fugitives did escape. If he did "organize the Massacre" as stated
by the *Encyclopaedia Britannica*, it must have been done
through the high confidence placed in him by the King—
verbally. On the evidence an impartial judge would have
to acquit him, or at least pass a verdict of "Not proven".

The verdicts passed by the Commission are easily dealt
with. The King was completely exonerated, and left to his
own conscience. The Address from the Scots Parliament gave
him a discharge in the most fulsome terms.

Stair was declared the author of the whole affair, and his
fate left to the King's mercy. William could scarcely deal

harshly with his Secretary while at the same time going free
from blame himself. So Stair resigned, or was retired, and
given a Scroll of Discharge (see Appendix XIII). The gift
of certain rents and feus in Glenluce from the King followed
his retiral in an almost indecently short space of time. In
November 1695 he became 2nd Viscount Stair on the death
of his father, and received an earldom in 1703. So he did not
suffer much. The best one can say for him is that from the
start he envisaged only a punitive expedition of a military
nature against the offending clans; but as plans matured some
others introduced the element of treachery which made it so
reprehensible. Who those others were it is impossible to
prove; but they must have been ones who had the necessary
local knowledge to formulate a plan of encirclement whereby
the MacIains could be trapped, and an intimate knowledge
of the customs of the Gael by the use of which troops could
be sent into the Glen and hospitably received until the time
came to strike. Argyll, Breadalbane and Hill all had that
knowledge; but which of them used it is matter for conjecture. It must have been one or all of them. Glenlyon was
only their tool.

Livingstone was acquitted, and raised to the peerage as
Viscount Teviot in 1696. In the New Year list of 1704 he
was made Lieutenant-General; and, when he died in 1711,
was accorded a fine funeral and buried in Westminster Abbey.

Colonel Sir John Hill was acquitted unreservedly.

Hamilton was judged guilty of murder, and the King asked
to prosecute. As we have seen he did not attend the inquiry,
but left for Ireland whence he went to the Army in Flanders.
Nothing was done to him. William needed all the soldiers he
could raise, and perhaps that was why the soldiers were not
sent home for trial.

All the others were judged guilty of "slaughter under
trust", the most serious indictment of all; and it was asked
that they be brought home from Flanders to stand trial.
Nothing was done and they never appeared. Duncanson, who
was certainly a good soldier, became a Lieutenant-Colonel
and fell honourably in action; but was never brought to trial.
Drummond, too, Glenlyon, Lindsay, Lundie, Barbour and
the rest of the soldiers continued to serve in Flanders and

were never tried. They just pursued the normal life of the soldier, gaining promotion as it came along, and no more said.

All these recommendations of the Commission and the Address to the King were made subject to the clause "as Your Majesty shall think fit". His Majesty did not think fit; and that was all about it. He could scarcely agree to act when he knew he was the fountain and origin of the whole dismal business, and yet had been acquitted with honour.

Some seem to have been granted "remission" for their deeds, Stair for one, and his came direct from the King (see Appendix XIII). A remission was actually a somewhat doubtful benefit, if a writer who seems to have had legal knowledge is to be believed. In 1703 there appeared in Edinburgh a pamphlet or circular in the form of notes added to an account of how the Report of the Duke of Hamilton's Commission had been suppressed in 1693. It is stated therein: "Some of the persons did get remission from K.W. concerning whom it is to be observed, first, that the taking of a remission is a tacit acknowledgement of the Crime, and taking upon them the guilt: Next, that any such remission is null and void, and will not defend them because it did not proceed upon letters of Slains (i.e. witnessing that the party wronged has received satisfaction) nor is there any Assithment (i.e. satisfaction) made to the nearest of kin; it being expressly by the Act 136, Par. 8. Jac. the 6th, that remissions are null unless the Party be assithed. . . . It is to be observed that the Parliament having declared that the killing of the Glenco-men was a Murder under Trust, Credit, Assurance and Power of the Slayer, is Treason: so by the said act, these that had accession to, or were anyways airt and part of the Slaying of the Glenco-men, are guilty of Treason.

"P.S. You know that there never was any prosecution against any of those persons charged with this barbarous murder, but that on the contrary, by the advice of some who were about H.M., several of the Officers were preferr'd, and the whole matter slurr'd over; so that the crying guilt of this blood must lie upon them and not upon the Nation, since Parliament could do no more in it without occasioning greater bloodshed than that they complain of. You know likewise that by the influence of the same persons this Report was suppressed in K.W.'s time, though H.M.'s honour required that it should have been published." (Scots Broadsides & Acts of Parl. 1689–1707.)

There it ends except that in certain quarters there was an outcry, especially from the Jacobites who demanded the blood of the criminals. Some very harsh things were said. and some very wild theories put forward. One pamphlet entitled "Gallienus Redivivus" sought to lay the blame on James Johnston, joint Secretary with Stair. Johnston was a staunch Protestant and Presbyterian, and the author of the "Gallienus" did not like Presbyterians; so, as Stair was quite impartial in matters of religion, Johnston had to be blamed without a shred of evidence. Letters of Johnston's show that he agreed with the King that action had to be taken, but was all against the manner in which it had been carried out. His letters show that his chief concern was to exculpate the Government, lay the blame on the Army, and use it as a weapon to attack the Stair family. He wrote to Carstairs: "I have the Glencoe affair in my hands with which I'll lash them into good behaviour cost what it will!" The other enemies of the Master and his father took advantage of the situation and Stair had to retire into the wilderness for a time, under advice from the King.

The verdict was brought in; but no sentences were ever passed. The Judge had other things on his mind; and, with that callousness of which he was capable, he occupied himself with matters which were, to him, far more important. As a counter-irritant he backed the Darien scheme, which followed hard on the heels of the Glencoe inquiry, but later he let the whole project fall into ruins through his fears of the vested interests of the English and Dutch companies. And very soon after that the Union of the Parliaments became the engrossing topic in Edinburgh and London. Glencoe was forgotten by all but those immediately concerned—the Jacobites and the Highlanders. Stair died amid the negotiations of the Union in 1707, but was not forgotten. Underneath all the activity of the period: the death of William, the accession of Anne, the Union of 1707, and all the political manœuvres connected with it, Glencoe still rankled; and the Rising of 1715 followed soon after the arrival of the "German lairdie", for whom the clans had less complimentary names. With the Massacre still fresh in their minds, and their memories of the last foreign king still green, they did not hesitate to take up arms again, in 1715, 1719 and 1745, the last desperate throw. Glencoe laid the foundations of them all.

By 1715 the Clann Iain had recovered in a wonderful way, and Alasdair, grandson of the murdered Chief, the babe who had been carried to safety in his nurse's arms, was able to raise nearly 100 fighting men, and a similar number in 1745, which shows how miserably the Massacre failed of its object.

In 1745 the MacIains were able to show true greatness of spirit when the Prince's Army lay at Kirkliston prior to their occupation of Edinburgh. "The Prince, in his anxiety to save Lord Stair from molestation, proposed that the Glencoe men should be marched to a distance from his residence, lest memories of ancient wrongs might move them to deeds of vengeance. When the proposal was made to the Glencoe men, their reply was that, if they were considered so dishonourable as to take revenge upon an innocent man, they were not fit to remain with honourable men, nor to support an honourable cause. It was only by much persuasion that they were induced to overlook what they regarded as an insult, and prevented from taking their departure" (*Clan Donald*, vol. 2). They stayed; but demanded that they should provide a guard to see that no harm came to the Dalrymple estate, lest they be blamed for it.

The "Glen of Weeping" has now become a resort under the care of the National Trust, and visitors are drawn to see the grandeur of its hills and to hear the story of the tragedy of that stormy morning of 13th February 1692, remembered by Highlanders for its callous violation of the ancient laws of hospitality—"Slaughter under Trust".

Appendix I

(See Chapter 5)

ARGYLL'S REGIMENT OF FOOT: ROLL OF OFFICERS APRIL 1689 AND OCTOBER 1691

THIS regiment was raised in April 1689 by the Earl of Argyll under a commission given by the Estates of Scotland. It was to have ten companies. Its composition was as follows:

Colonel The Earl of Argyll   *Lieut.-Col.* Duncan Campbell
Major Robert Duncanson   of Achinbreck

Captains (*Company Commanders*)
Aulay Macaulay of Ardin-   James Campbell, Yr. of Ard-
caple   kinglas
Archibald Lamont   Archibald Campbell of Torrie
Archibald Campbell of Bar- Hector Bannatyne, Yr. of
breck   Kaimes
Robert Campbell of Glenlyon

The Muster Rolls nearest to the time of the Massacre are those of October 1691 when there are 13 Companies of 64 men, including officers, in each, except for Argyll's own company which had 72, making a total of 840. The establishment at that time was as follows:

Colonel The Earl of Argyll   *Lieut.-Col.* Jackson
Major Robert Duncanson

Captains (*Company Commanders*)
David Bruce   Duncan Campbell of Kaimes
James Campbell, Yr. of Ard- John Campbell of Airds
kinglas   Neill Campbell
John Campbell   Thomas Drummond
Robert Campbell of Glenlyon John Campbell
Aulay Macaulay

It is to be noted that there are some 90 men of all ranks of the name of Campbell, and numerous others of names of clans allied to the House of Argyll. In the whole regiment there were three Macdonalds and two MacEacherns, making only five men of Clan Donald, contrary to some sources which state that Macdonalds participated in the massacre of their fellow clansmen. One was in Duncanson's Coy., and two in John Campbell's.

At this time there is no mention of the Lindsays in Glenlyon's company; but there is a John Lindsay listed as Aide-Major in the Earl's own Headquarter Company; and another John Lindsay a Lieutenant in the Company of Captain Duncan Campbell of Kaimes. The name "Lundie" is mentioned in some accounts (instead of Lindsay) as the Ensign of Glenlyon's Company. The name appears at this time (October 1691) as an Ensign in Captain David Bruce's Company. By the time of the Massacre there may, of course, have been transfers made from one company to another. In October 1691 Glenlyon's Lieutenant was John Millon, and his Ensign was a John Campbell (see Muster Roll of Glenlyon's Company in Appendix IV).

Major Duncanson, at that time a Captain, had accompanied the 9th Earl of Argyll on his ill-fated expedition in 1685, and was with him to the end, escaping narrowly. He was very much Argyll's man and loyal supporter.

Appendix II

(See Chapter 5)

COLONEL HILL'S REGIMENT: MUSTER ROLL,
JANUARY 1692. OFFICERS AND COUNT OF SOLDIERS
(MACDONALDS ONLY)

Hill's Company (H.Q.)
William Richardson Capt.
William Garvan Quarter-
Master
John Munro Surgeon-Major

Major John Forbes (bro. of
Culloden)
Walter Drummond Ensign
Duncan Buchanan Adjutant
Lt.-Col. James Hamilton

Company Commanders—Captains
James Cunningham
Lord Kilmairs
James Munro
John Stewart
Charles Forbes

John Mackenzie
Alexander Stevenson
Robert Hunter
John McCulloch
James Stewart

10 Companies of 88 men (average)
Note: In Lt.-Col. Hamilton's Company the Lieutenant was
James Hamilton
John Campbell Lieut.   James Simpson Ensign
John and Alexander Hamilton—Sergeants
John Campbell, John Auld, and William Arnott were the
Corporals.
Of the soldiers two were Campbells, one Macdonald (Alan),
and one Cameron.
The composition of this company is mentioned as it was one
of those of Hill's Regiment directly concerned in the
Massacre.

Because of wild statements by some (Campbells and others)
that the Massacre was carried out by Macdonalds against
Macdonalds, a search was made for all possible members of

Clan Donald serving in the companies involved. The Muster Rolls reveal only three Macdonalds and two MacEacherns in the whole of Argyll's Regiment, and one Macdonald in the Company of Hill's employed by Hamilton. In Glenlyon's company there are two MacEacherns, who might be regarded as members Clan of Donald. (See Appendix IV.)

Appendix III

(See Chapter 7)

NOTES ON THE KING'S SIGNATURE (TWICE) ON THE ORDER FOR THE MASSACRE

RE the King's action in superscribing and subscribing the orders for the Massacre, which by many has been construed as showing that the King made very sure his orders would be obeyed, Sir William Fraser in *The Annandale Family Book*, Vol. 1, pp. cclxxxii to cclxxxiv defends the King's action, as being no wise out of the ordinary. He writes:

"Blame has frequently been thrown upon King William because his formal instructions to Sir Thomas Livingstone, commander in chief of the forces in Scotland, to carry out the military executions against Glencoe were both 'superscribed' and 'subscribed' by him. On 11th January, Sir John Dalrymple in a relative letter of that date, specially draws attention of Sir Thomas Livingstone to this feature of the royal warrant, evidently for the purpose of possessing him with the idea of the strong desire of the king to have the military executions carried out with rigour and zeal. This feature of the royal warrant and the pointed reference to it by the Master of Stair, whatever the effect it had upon Sir Thomas Livingstone, has undoubtedly conveyed the impression to subsequent historians and to the public generally, desired by the Secretary of State, namely, an impression of the king's determination to root out the Highland rebels." He then refers to Sir Walter Scott's *Tales of a Grandfather*, where reference is made to this "remarkable" fact, and its importance. Sir William goes on: "Great injustice has been done to King William by the misrepresentation of the facts on this particular point. The king did not, as has been supposed, depart in the least from the course he usually followed in subscribing royal warrants

when he superscribed and sub-initialled his instructions to Sir
Thomas Livingstone on 11th January 1692, and also his additional instructions to him on the 16th of the same month. The
practice of the sovereigns of England was to superscribe all
royal warrants. On the other hand, that of the sovereigns of
Scotland was to subscribe them. King James the Sixth, after
his accession to the throne of England, King Charles the
First, and King Charles the Second all followed the English
practice of superscribing warrants. King William followed
the same course of superscribing his name in full, but also
very commonly with the addition of writing his initials of
'W.R.' at the foot of the warrant. The Earl of Melvill, the
first secretary of state for Scotland under William, received
many warrants and instructions under the hand of the King,
bearing his full name 'William R.' superscribed at the top
and his initials 'W.R.' at the foot. Occasionally when the
king superscribed in full, and did not add his initials at the
foot of the warrant, the secretary of state subscribed his name
in place of the royal initials."

Sir William Fraser then adds several examples of this
double signing of a warrant by the King—some to General
Mackay, others to Melvill.

Appendix IV

(See Chapter 8)

MUSTER ROLL OF GLENLYON'S COMPANY OF ARGYLL'S REGIMENT 23RD OCTOBER 1691

Captain Robert Campbell of Glenlyon
Ensign John Campbell
Drummers Mungo Dalzell and Cuthbert Hunter

Lieutenant John Millon
Sergeants Robert Barbour and James Hendrie
N.B.—No pipers mentioned.

Section 1

Archibald Campbell (Corp.)
Archibald Gray
Archibald Campbell
Adam McCoy?
Alexander Miln
Archibald Blaire
Archibald MacConnay?
Archibald Morison
Archibald Macinkerd?

Andrew Gray
Archibald MacLeane
Donald Campbell Sr.
Donald Campbell Yr.
Donald MacCallum Sr.
Donald MacCallum Yr.
Donald Mac—?
Donald Mackinlayroy
Donald Richardson

Section 2

James McPhell (Corp.)
Duncan McCallum
Duncan McPhell
Duncan Maclachland
Duncan McKinlayroy
Duncan McKerracher
Duncan Campbell
Duncan Robertson
George Campbell
Henry Dyall

James Campbell
John MacDugall
John Dunbar
John MacKerracher
John MacCulloch
Duncan Macnachtan
John Ferguson
John George
Duncan MacCallum Yr.
John MacKinley

139

Section 3

Duncan Kennedie (Corp.)
John Mackechirn
John Stewart
John Turner
John McCallum
John Alexander
Loo Robertson
Malcolm Sinclair
Malcolm MacCulloch
Malcolm Robertson

Malcolm MacClean
Morton Mackinvin
Malcolm Gillos
Patrick MacIntyre
Patrick MacKechern
Robert Peatrie
Thomas Bruntfield
Thomas Stott
Edward Oboey?
Walter Gilroy

Appendix V

(See Chapter 8)

LULLABY OF THE SNOW (*Taladh an t-sneachda*)

THE poem (below) was taken down by John MacNab, student of divinity, from Big Peter Macdonald in Glencoe.

The night after the massacre of Glencoe officers and soldiers were sent out searching the hills for any stray fugitives who might have escaped the massacre. Hearing the sound of a bagpipe, they followed it, thinking it might be some Macdonald guiding his friends to safety. Eager to wreak their vengeance on the clan they hated, they followed the piping through mud and mire, swamp and stream, till they reached a distant tarn among the high mountains. Here the music sank down into the depths of the tarn and died softly away as dies the eerie sough of the west wind. The people (of the Glen) maintain that the piper was one of the good fairies of the mound.

Beaten and battered by the storm, with baffled rage in their hearts and curses on their lips, the soldiers returned. They heard upon the wind the screaming of a child. The officer in command called out to the nearest soldier, "Go and put a twist in the neck of that brat!" As the man made for the place from which the screams were coming, he heard the most beautiful music he had ever heard. Who was this but a young mother who had escaped lulling her child to sleep—the sleep of death. The soldier remembered her whom he had left at home with a little babe at her breast, crooning to him, and the blood of Clan Donald in the veins of both. And it chanced that the gentle croon of music that the child's mother sang was the very music he had last heard when he left home any a day and year before. The soldier wrapped the woman and her child in his plaid, gave them what food he had, and left

them to overtake his comrades. On the way he came upon a
wolf devouring the body of a woman. He slew the wolf and
showed the officer the blood on his sword. By the mercy of
God and through the soldiers' compassion mother and child
survived. Descendants of the child are still living, and the
tradition is believed throughout the districts of Appin and
Lochaber.

The song the woman sang is as follows:

Is fuar, fuar an nochd mo leaba	Cold, cold this night is my bed.
Is fuar, fuar an nochd mo leanabh	Cold, cold this night is my child.
Is buan, buan an nochd do chadal	Lasting, lasting this night thy sleep.
Mis 'am anart 's tus' am achlais	I in my shroud and thou in my arm.
Tha sgàil a' bhàis a' snàgan tharam	The shadow of death creeps o'er me.
Cuisle blath mo ghràidh cha caraich	The warm pulse of my love will not stir.
Gaoth na ard do thàladh cadail	The wind of the heights thy sleep-lulling.
Sneachd nam beann gu teann do bhrata	The close-clinging snow of the peaks thy mantle.

There are many more verses.

This has been copied from Carmina Gadelica by Carmichael
with the permission of the executors and heirs of the late
Professor J. C. Watson.

Appendix VI

(See Chapter 8)

WORDS SET TO BREADALBANE'S MARCH (Pibroch)

THE words said to have been conveyed by Breadalbane's March, the pibroch composed at Allt nam Meirleach, now used as a warning to the people of Glencoe by Glenlyon's piper were

> *'Mhuinntir a' ghlinne so, ghlinne so, ghlinne so*
> *'s mithich dhuibh eirigh!*
> Folk of this Glen, you had better be rising!

On these words the late Neil Macleod composed a song which is popular today, and is often sung at ceilidhs.

'Mhuinntir a' ghlinne so, Ghlinne so, ghlinne so, 's mithich dhuibh eirigh.
Rinn iad ar mealladh, ar mealladh, ar mealladh,
Gu'n d'rinn iad ar mealladh le geallanna breugach;
'Mithich dhuibh gluasad 's na tighean nan luaithre,
's ur companaich shuairce 'nan suain as nach eirigh,
'Nan laidh' air an urlar gun aighear, gun sugradh,
's an fhuil a bha muirneach gu siubhlach o'n creuchdan.

Tha osag nam fuar-bheann ri aghaidh nan cruachan
A' caoidh nam fear uasal a' bhuaileadh le eucoir;
Craobh mhullaich Chloinn Domhnaill chaidh ghearradh le
*   foirneart,*
's am meanganan oga gun treoir air an reubadh.
Le tuirse no tuireadh cha duisgear iad tuilleadh
Gu'n crionar an cruinne cha'n urrainn iad eirigh.
Gu'n teirig na beanntan bidh cuimhne air a ghleann so
's air toradh a' ghamhlais 'us feall an luchd-reubadh.

From: *A' Choisir-chiuil* (Bayley and Ferguson)
and other sources.

Appendix VII

(See Chapter 9)

LETTER FROM A GENTLEMAN IN EDINBURGH TO
HIS FRIEND IN LONDON AFTER THE MASSACRE

Edinburgh   April 20th 1692

Sir,

The account you desired of that strange and surprizing Massacre of Glencoe take as follows:

Mac-Ian Mac-donald, Laird of Glenco, a branch of the Mackdonalds, one of the greatest Clans (or Tribes) in the North of Scotland, came with the most considerable men of his Clan to Coll. Hill, Governour of Fort William at Inverlochy, some few days before the expiring of the time for receiving the indemnity appointed by the proclamation, which as I take it, was the first of January last, entreating he would administer unto him the oaths which the foresaid proclamation required to be taken; that so submitting himself to the Government, he might have its protection. The Colonel received him with all expressions of kindness; nevertheless shifted the administering the Oaths to him, alledging that by the Proclamation it did not belong to him, but to the Sheriffs, Bailiffs of Regalities, and Magistrates of Burghs, to administer them. MacIan complaining that by this disappointment he might be wronged, the time being now near expiring, and the weather so extreme, and the ways so very bad, that it was not possible for him so soon to reach any Sheriff, etc. got from Coll. Hill, under his hand, his protection; and withal he was assured, that no orders from the Government against him should be put into execution, until he were first advertised, and had time allowed him to apply himself to King or Council for his safety. But the better to make all sure (tho' this might have seemed security enough for that time) with all despatch imaginable he posted to Inverary, the Chief Town of Argyleshire, there he found Sir Collin Campbell of Ardkinlis, Sheriff of the Shire, and craved of him the benefit of the indemnity, according to the Proclamation, he being willing to perform all the conditions required. Sir Collin at first scrupled to admit him to the oaths, the time which the Proclamation did appoint being elapsed by one day, alledging it would be of no use to him then to take them: but MacIan represented that it was not his fault, he having come in time enough to Coll. Hill, not doubting but he could have administered the oaths to him, and that upon his refusal he had made such hast to Inverary, that he might have come in time enough, had not the extremity of the weather hindered him; and even as it was, he was but one day after the time appointed; and that would be very unbecoming the Government to take advantage of a man's coming late by one day, especially when he had done his utmost to have come in time. Upon this, and his threatening to protest against the Sheriff for the severity of his usage, he administered to him and his attendants the oaths, MacIan depending upon the indemnity granted to those who should take them; and having so done, he went home, and lived quietly and peaceably under the Government, till the day of his death.

In January last, a party of the Earl of Argile's Regiment came to that country; the design of their coming was then suspected to be to take course with those who should stand out and not submit and take the oaths. The garrison of Inverlochy being thronged, and Glenco being commodious for quartering, as being near the garrison, those soldiers were sent thither to quarter; they pretended they came to exact arrears of cess and hearth-money (a tax never known in Scotland, until laid on by the Parliament, 1690, after the Parliament of England had eased themselves of it) e'er they entered Glenco, that Laird or his sons came out to meet them, and asked them if they came as friends or enemies? The Officers answered as friends; and gave their Paroll of Honour that they would do neither him nor his concerns any harm; upon which he welcomed them, promising them the best entertainment the place could afford. This he really performed, as all the soldiers confess. He and they lived together in mutual kindness and friendship fifteen days or thereabouts; so far was he from fearing any hurt from them. And the very last day of his life he spent in keeping company with the commander of that party, Capt. Campbell of Glenlyon, playing at cards with him till 6 or 7 at night, and at their parting mutual protestations of kindness were renewed. Some time that very day, but whether before or after their parting, I know not, Capt. Campbell had these orders sent him by Major Duncanson, a copy of which I here send you.

Ballacholis. Feb 12th 1692

Sir,

You are hereby ordered to fall upon the rebels the Mac-Donalds of Glenco, and put all to the sword under 70. You are to have especial care that the Old Fox and his sons do upon no account escape your hands; you are to secure all the avenues that no man escape: This you are to put in execution at five a clock in the morning precisely, and by that time or very shortly after I'll strive to be at you with a stronger party; If I do not come to you at five, you are not to tarry for me, but to fall on. This is by the Kings Special Command, for the good and safety of the country, that those miscreants may be cut off, root and branch. See that this be put in execution without feud or favour, else you may expect to be treated as not true to the King or Government, not a man fit to carry Commission in the King's service. Expecting you will not fail in the fulfilling hereof, as you love yourself. I subscribe these with my hand,

Robert Duncanson

"For their Majesties Service, to Cap. Robert Campbell of Glenlyon."

Duncanson had received orders from Lieutenant Collonel Hamilton, which were as follows:

Ballacholis. Feb. 12 1692

Sir,

Per second to the Commander in Chief, and my Colonel's orders to me, for putting in execution the service commanded against the rebels in Glenco, wherein you, with the party of the Earl of Argyle's Regiment under your command are to be concerned: You are therefore forthwith to order your affairs so, as that the several posts already assigned you, be by you and your several detachments fallen in action with, precisely by five o'clock tomorrow morning, being Saturday: at which time I will endeavour the same with those appointed from this regiment for the other places. It will be most necessary you secure those avenues on the South side, that the Old Fox, nor none of his Cubs get away. The orders are that none be spared, from 70, of the sword, nor the Government troubled with prisoners. This is all, until I see you.

From　　　　　　　Your humble servant,
　　　　　　　　　　　　　　James Hamilton.

Please to order a guard to secure the ferry, and the boats there; and the boats must be all on this side the ferry after your men are over.

　　"For their Majesties Service, for Major Robert
　　　　Duncanson, of the Earl of Argyle's Regiment."

The soldiers being disposed five or three in a house, according to the number of the family they were to assassinate, had their orders given them secretly. They had been received as friends by those poor people, who intended no evil themselves, and little suspected that their guests were designed to be their murtherers. At 5 o'clock in the morning they began their bloody work, surprised and butchered 38 persons who had kindly received them under their roofs. MacIan himself was murthered and is much bemoaned. He was a stately well-favoured man and of good courage and sense; As also the Laird of Archintrikin, a gentleman of more than ordinary judgment and understanding, who had submitted to the Government, and had Coll. Hill's protection in his pocket, which he had got three months before. I cannot without horror represent how that a boy of eight years of age was murthered: he seeing what was done to others in the house with him, in a terrible fright ran out of the house, and espying Capt. Campbell, grasped him about the legs, crying for mercy, and offering to be his servant for life. I am informed Capt. Campbell inclined to spare him; but one Drummond, an officer, barbarously ran his dagger through him whereof he died immediately. The rehearsal of several particulars and circumstances of this tragical story makes it appear most doleful; as that MacIan was killed as he was drawing on his breeches, standing before his bed, and giving orders to his servants for the good entertainment of those who murthered him; While he was speaking the words he was shot through the head and fell dead in his lady's arms, who through the grief of this and other bad usages she met with, died the next day. It is not to be omitted that most of these poor people were killed when they were asleep and none allowed to pray to God for mercy. Providence ordered it so that that night was most boisterous; so as a party of 400 men who should have come to the other end of the glen, and begun the like work there at the same hour (intending that the poor inhabitants should be enclosed and none of them escape) could not march at length until it was 9 o'clock and this afforded to many an opportunity of escaping and none were killed but those in whose houses Glenlyon's men were quartered, otherwise all the males under 70 years of age to the number of 200 had been cut off, for that was the order; and it might have been easily executed, especially considering that the inhabitants had no arms at the time; for upon first hearing that the soldiers were coming to the Glen, they had conveyed them all out of the way: For though they relied on the promises which were made them for their safety, yet they thought it not improbable that they might be disarmed. I know not whether to impute it to difficulty of distinguishing the difference of a few years, or to the fury of the soldiers, who being once glutted with blood, stand at nothing, that even some above seventy years of age were destroyed. They set fire to all the houses, drove off all the cattle to the garrison of Inverlochy, viz. 900 cows, 200 horses, and a great many sheep and goats, and there they were divided amongst the officers. And how dismal may you imagine the case of the poor women and children was then! It was lamentable past expression, their husbands and fathers and near relations were forced to flee for their lives; they themselves almost stript, and nothing left them, and their houses being burnt, and not one house nearer than six miles; and to get thither they were to pass over mountains, wreaths of snow, in a vehement storm, wherein the greatest part of them perished through hunger and cold. It fills me with horror to think of poor stript children and women, some with child, and some giving suck, wrestling against a storm in mountains and heaps of snow, and at length overcome, and give over, and fall down and die miserably.

You see in Hamilton's orders to Duncanson there's a special caution, That the Old Fox nor none of his cubs should escape; and in Duncanson's order to Capt. Campbell of Glenlyon, That the Old Fox nor none of his sons escape; but notwithstanding all this wicked caution, it pleased God that the two young Gentlemen, MacIan's sons escaped: for it happened that the younger of these gentlemen trusted little to the fair promises of Campbell, and had a more watchful eye over him than his father or brother, who suffered themselves by his reiterated oaths to be deluded into a belief of his integrity: he having a strong impression on his spirit that some mischievous design was hidden under Campbell's specious promises, it made him, after the rest were in bed, remain in a retired corner, where he had an advantagious prospect into their guard. About midnight perceiving several soldiers to enter it, this encreased his jealousy; so he went and communicated his fears to his brother, who could not for a long time be persuaded there was any bad design against them, and asserted that what he had seen was not a doubling their guards in order to any ill design, but that being in a strange place and at a distance from the garrison, they were to send our centinels far from the guard, and because of the extremity of the weather relieved them often, and the men he saw could be no more than these. Yet he persisting to say, that they were not so secure, but that it was fit to acquaint their father with what he had seen, he prevailed with his brother to rise, and go with him to his father who lay in a room contiguous to that they were in. Though what the younger son alledged made no great impression on his father, yet he allowed his sons to try what they could discover. They well knowing all the skulking places there, went and hid themselves near to a centinel's post, where instead of one they found eight or ten men; this made them more inquisitive, so they crept as near as they could without being

discovered so near that they could hear one say to his
fellows, That he liked not this work, and that had he known
of it he would have been very unwilling to have come here;
but that none, except their commanders, knew of it until
within a quarter of an hour. The soldier added, That he was
willing to fight against the men of the Glen, but it was base to
murder them. But to all this was answered, All the blame be
on such as gave the orders; we are free, being bound to obey
our officers. Upon hearing of these words the young gentlemen retired as quickly and quietly as they could towards the
house, to inform their father of what they had heard; but as
they came nigh to it, they perceived it surrounded and guns
discharged, and the people shrieking, whereupon being un-
armed and totally unable to rescue their father, they preserved their own lives in hopes yet to serve their King and
country, and see Justice done upon those Hell-hounds,
treacherous murtherers, the shame of their country, and
disgrace of Mankind.

I must not forget to tell you, That there were two of these
officers who had given their paroll of honour to MacIan, who
refused to be concerned in that brutal tragedy, for which
they were sent prisoners to Glasgow, where if they remain
still I am sure they were some weeks ago.

Thus, Sir, in obedience to your commands, I have sent you
such account as I could get of that monstrous and most
inhuman massacre of the Laird of Glenco, and others of his
clan. You desire some proof of the truth of the story, for you
say there are many in England who cannot believe such a thing
could be done, and publick Justice not executed upon the
ruffians: for they take it for granted that no such order could
be given by the Government; and you say they will never
believe it without a downright demonstration. Sir, As to the
Government, I will not meddle with it; or whether these
officers who murdered Glenco, had such orders as they pretended from the Government, the Government knows that
best, and how to vindicate their own honour, and punish the
murtherers who pretended their authority and still stand
upon it. But as to the matter of fact of the murder of Glenco,
you may depend upon it as certain and undeniable. It would
be thought as strange a thing in Scotland for any man to

doubt of it, as of the death of my Lord Dundee, or with you
that the Duke of Monmouth lost his head. But, to put you
out of all doubt, you will e'er long have my Lord Argyle's
Regiment with you in London, and there you may speak with
Glenlyon himself, with Drummond and the rest of the actors
in that dismal tragedy; and on my life, there is never a one
of them will deny it to you; for they know that it is notoriously
known all over Scotland, and it is an admiration to us that
there should be anyone in England who makes the least doubt
of it. Nay, Glenlyon is so far from denying it, that he brags
of it, and justifies his action publicly; He said in the Royal
Coffee House in Edinburgh that he would do it again, nay,
that he would stab any man in Scotland or in England without asking the cause, if the King gave him orders, and that it
was every good subject's duty so to do; and I am reliably
informed that Glenlyon and the rest of them have addressed
themselves to the Council for a reward for their good service
in destroying Glenco, pursuant to their orders.

There is enough of this mournful subject: if what I have
said satisfy you not, you may have what further proof and
in what manner you please to ask it.

Sir, Your humble servant, etc. . . .

NOTE: That the gentleman to whom this letter was sent,
did on Thursday June 30th 1692. when Argyle's Regiment
was quartered at Brentford, go thither and had this story of
the Massacre of Glenco from the very men who were the
actors in it: Glenlyon and Drummond were both there.
The Highlander who told him the story expressing guilt
which was visible in Glenlyon, said, Glenco hangs about
Glenlyon night and day: you may see him in his face. I am
told likewise that Sir John Lowther refused to accept of the
place of Lord Advocate of Scotland unless he might have
liberty to prosecute Glenlyon and the rest of the murtherers
of Glenco, which not being granted James Stuart (who was
forfeited for treason by K.C.2. and since knighted by K.W.)
has now the place.

Appendix VIII

(See Chapter 10)

LETTER FROM ANNANDALE TO HILL (SUMMONS TO ATTEND) AND HIS REPLY

Edinburgh, 23rd May 1695

Sir, It hath pleased his majestie to give a commission under the broad seall to the Marquis of Tweeddale, the Earle of Annandale, and sevein more, to take tryall by what warrands and in what manner the Glenco men were killed in February 1692, and for that end to call for all persons, letter and other writings that may give any light in it; as also to call and examine witnesses upon oath that there may be a full discovery, and the whole reported to His Majesty. Which commission being now met, I am by them appointed to require yow to come to Edinburgh to attend them with all possible diligence, and that yow bring with yow all instructions, orders, missive letters, or other writings that ye have about that affair, and that yow bring the principals and not copies attested by your hand. As likewayes yow are to bring with yow the persons that yow can command or influence who were present at the execution, or who can give any knowledge of the contrivance and manadgment of that affair, or of any part of it, and who see old Glencoe with yow at Fort William in December 1691 or January 1962, and who can witness what passed at that time. In these things yow are to show your care and diligence that the enquiry may be made and despatched as is expected. Sir Thomas Livingstone is to write to yow to this purpose, and to send Lieutenant Collonell Jackson to command in your absence, which is all at present that the commission ordered to be signified to yow by, sir, your humble servant,

Annandale P.

When I speak of these that were present at the execution, I mean only a sufficient number, as sevein or eight of those that know the matter best.

For Collonell Hill, Governour of Fort William.

Colonel John Hill to William, Earl of Annandale.

My Lord, I haue your lordship's order of the 23rd of this month, to which I shall giue all ready obedience, takeing only two days to setle affairs, and giue the necessary order (Lieutenant-Colonell Jackson beinge a strange here). I shall bringe such of the officers as are upon the place, many of them beinge abroad aboute getting up recruits. The person (that by the major-generalls order was appoynted to command the partie that went at that tyme to Glenco, and comanded the wholl) is Lieutenant-Colonell James Hamilton, who, I hear, is now in Ireland. I resolue (if God please) to sett out betymes, on Monday morning, and to be at Edinburgh as soone as possibly I can, who am, my Lord, your lordship's most humble and obedient servant,

Jo. Hill.

Fort William, 30th may 1695.

These two letters (Annandale to Hill, and Hill's reply) are taken from *The Annandale Family Book*, Vol. 2, pp. 116 and 54 respectively. In that book the second letter is dated 30th May 1692; but, as it is very plainly the answer to Annandale's summons to Hill to attend, it is assumed that it is really of date 30th May 1695.

Appendix IX

(See Chapter 10)

LT.-COL. JAMES HAMILTON'S LETTER OF EXCUSE FOR ABSENTING HIMSELF FROM THE INQUIRY

5th July 1695

My Lord,

My unhappy circumstances at present I hope will excuse this boldness I take to give your lordship this trouble.

I have not the least doubt of the justice and tender consideration that should be shown me in that my unfortunat affaire before the honorable high court of Parliament, but that there runs such a speat and odium cast on me, that I haue not been injenious in declaring the truth accordin to my knowledg; in which I call to witness the Almighty God, judge of all men's hearts and actions, that I haue from the sincerity of my soule, done it both in discourse to the secretary and others of my sentiments of the matter, as well as discharged my conscience upon my oath in matter of fact. I likewyse utterly deny upon the faith of a Christian hauing anything to do with a party as is alledged, or ever had, more than became me or a person of my station in duety and sivility, which I thought I had practised to all mankinde.

My Lord, the denyell of copies attested of my papers given in to the Commission notwithstanding your lordships ordered the clearke to do it, with many other discourses proceeding from some members of that commission and the parliament, hath given rise to all my jeilousyes and feares, and the only occasion of this my absenting. I again implore the Almighty God to judge of my inocency. I begg your lordships and the members Christian charity, and shall hope for their judicious consideration of all, which I pray the Lord direct them in. And as I presumed to address your lordship last winter for your favour and recomendation, soo I most humbly continue the same, that I may haue access to the King, where and to whom I will declare the whole of what I haue discoursed the secretary. or what I can say, and thus relyeing on your lordships and the parliaments tender consideration and most humbly begging pardon for this transgression of abcenting,

I ever shall remain with all submition, my lord, your lordships

most humble and obedient servant,

Ja. Hamilton.

For the right honourable the Earle of Annandale, lord precedent of his majesties high court of parliament now sitting in Edinburgh.

(From *The Annandale Family Book*, by Sir William Fraser, K.C.B., LL.D., Vol. 2, page 118.)

Appendix X

(See Chapter 10)

COMMISSION FROM THE KING TO SET UP INQUIRY

WILLIAM, by the Grace of God, King of Great Britain, &c.—
To all good men to whom these presents shall come, greeting:
Whereas we have taken into consideration, that though in
the year of our Lord 1693, we gave power, by express
instructions, to William Duke of Hamilton, deceased, and
others, to examine and enquire into the slaughter of certain
people of the name of Macdonald, and others, in Glenco, in
the year 1692, and into the way and manner how the same
was committed; yet, nevertheless, the enquiry then made,
pursuant to the said instructions, was defective; and considering likewise, that the most effectual method for receiving full information of the true circumstances of the matter
aforesaid, must be by a commission to that effect; and being
very well satisfied of the abilities and fitness of the persons
under named, for the ends above expressed; know ye therefore, that we have named and constituted, and by the tenor
of these presents, do name and constitute, our right trusty
and well-beloved cousin and councellor, John Marquis of
Tweddale, our high chancellor, and William Earl of Anan-
dale, and our trusty and beloved councellors John Lord
Murray, Sir James Stuart, our advocate, Adam Cockburn
of Ormiston, our Justice-Clerk, Mr Archibald Hope of
Rankeiller, and Sir William Hamilton of Whitelaw, Senators
of our College of Justice, Sir James Ogilvy, our solicitor, and
Adam Drummond of Meggins, (of whom five shall be a
quorum, and granting them power to chuse their own clerk),
our commissioners, to take precognition and make inquiry
into the slaughter aforesaid, by whom, and how, and by what
colour of authority, the same was committed: and in order

to the discovery of the same, we give power to the said commissioners to send for all warrants and directions granted for that end; and also to examine all persons that had any hand in the business aforesaid, and likewise to examine witnesses as shall be found necessary, either upon oath or declaration; and afterwards the said commissioners shall transmit to us the true state of the matter aforesaid, together with the proofs and evidence that shall be brought before them, that after due and full information, we may give such directions thereupon, as to us shall seem meet and necessary. In testimony whereof, we have commanded our great seal to be appended to these presents.

Given at our Court of Kensington, the 29th day of April 1695, and of our reign the seventh.

Superscribed by the signature of the hand writing of our most Serene Lord the King.

Written to the Great Seal, and Registered the 20th day of May 1695.

Don Rannald, Deput.
Sealed at Edinburgh, May 20, 1695.
Jo. Dicksone.

presented to Parliament.

Upon the 23d of May 1695, this commission was read in Parliament, and the House voted, nemine contradicente, that his Majesty's high commissioner transmit the humble thanks of the Parliament to his Majesty, for ordering an enquiry into that matter, whereby the honour and justice of the nation might be vindicated.

It being urged that the commission should proceed with diligence, as being a national concern, and that the discovery be made known to the House before its adjournment, his Grace assured them, that he doubted not of his Majesty's giving satisfaction to his Parliament in that point, and that before they parted.

The commissioners proceeded according to order, and made the following report.

Appendix XI

(See Chapter 10)

REPORT OF THE COMMISSION GIVEN BY HIS MAJESTY
FOR INQUIRING INTO THE SLAUGHTER OF THE MEN
OF GLENCO, SUBSCRIBED AT HALYRUD-HOUSE, THE
20TH DAY OF JUNE 1695

JOHN Marquis of Tweddale, Lord High Chancellor of
Scotland, William Earl of Annandail, John Lord Murray, Sir
James Stuart, his Majesty's advocate, Adam Cockburn of
Ormistoun, Lord Justice-Clerk, Sir Archibald Hope of
Rankeillor, and Sir William Hamilton of Whitelaw, two of
the Senators of the College of Justice, Sir James Ogilvy, his
Majesty's Solicitor, and Adam Drummond of Megginsh,
commissioners appointed by his Majesty, by his commission
under the great seal, of the date the 29th of April last, to make
enquiry, and to take trial and precognition about the slaughter
of several persons of the sirname of Macdonald, and others, in
Glenco, in the year 1692, by whom, and in what manner, and
by what pretended authority, the same was committed, with
power to call for all warrants and directions given in that
matter; as also to examine all persons who had a hand therein,
with what witnesses they should find necessary, either upon
oath or declaration, and to report to his Majesty the true
state of the said matter, with the evidence and testimonies to
be adduced before them, as the said commission more amply
bears. Having met and qualified themselves by taking the
oath of allegiance and assurance, conform to the act of Parliament, with the oath de fideli, as use is in such cases, did,
according to the power given to them, chuse Mr Alexander
Monro of Beircroft to be their clerk, and he having also
qualified himself as above, they proceeded into the said
enquiry, to call for all warrants and directions, with all such

persons as witnesses, that might give light in the said matter; and having considered the foresaid warrants and directions produced before them, and take the oaths and depositions of the witnesses under-named, they, with all submission, lay the report of the whole discovery made by them before his Majesty in the order following. And, first, of somethings that preceded the said slaughter: secondly, of the matter of fact, with the proofs and evidence taken, when and in what manner the same was committed: thirdly, of the warrants and directions that either really were, or were pretended, for the committing it: and, lastly, the commissioners humble opinion of the true state and account of that whole business.

The things to be remarked preceding the said slaughter were, that it's certain that the Lairds of Glenco and Auchintriaten, and their followers, were in the insurrection and rebellion made by some of the Highland clans, under the command first of the Viscount Dundee, and then of Major General Buchan, in the years 1689 and 1690. This is acknowledged by all. But when the Earl of Braidalbine called the heads of the clans, and met with them in Auchallader in July 1691, in order to a cessation, the deceased Alexander Macdonald of Glenco was there, with Glengary, Sir John Maclene, and others, and agreed to the cessation, as it is also acknowledged: but the deceased Glenco's two sons, who were at that time with their father in the town of Auchallader, depone, that they heard that the Earl of Braidalbine did at that time quarrel with the deceased Glenco about some cows, that the Earl alleged were stolen from his men by Glenco's men; and that though they were not present to hear the words, yet their father told them of the challenge; and the two sons, with Ronald Macdonald, indweller in Glenco, and Ronald Macdonald in Innerriggin, in Glenco, do all depone, that they heard the deceased Glenco say, that the Earl of Braidalbine, at the meeting of Auchallader, threatened to do him a mischief, and that he feared a mischief from no man so much as from the Earl of Braidalbine, as their depositions at the letter A in the margin bears. And Alexander Macdonald, second son to the deceased Glenco, doth farther depone, that he hath often heard from his father and others, that there had been in former times blood betwixt Braidalbine's family and their clan, as his deposition at the same mark bears. And here the commissioners cannot but take notice of what hath occurred to them in two letters from Secretary Stair to Lieutenant-Colonel Hamilton, one of the first, and another of the third of December 1691, wherein he expresses his resentment "for the marring of the bargain that should have been betwixt the Earl of Braidalbine and the Highlanders, to a very great hight, charging some for their despite against him, as if it had been the only hindrance of that settlement." Whence he goes on in his of the third December to say, "That since the government cannot oblige them, it is obliged to ruine some of them to weaken and frighten the rest, and that the Macdonalds will fall in this net." And, in effect, seems even from that time, which was almost a month before the expiring of the king's indemnity, to project with Lieutenant-Colonel Hamilton, that some of them should be rooted out and destroyed. His Majesty's proclamation of indemnity was published in August 1691, offering a free indemnity and pardon to all the Highlanders who had been in arms, upon their coming in and taking the oath of allegiance, betwixt and the first of January thereafter. And in compliance with the proclamation, the deceased Glenco goes about the end of December 1691, to Colonel Hill, governor of Fort-William at Inverlochie, and desired the Colonel to minister to him the oath of allegiance, that he might have the king's indemnity. But Colonel Hill, in his deposition, marked with the letter B. doth farther depone, That he hastened him away all he could, and gave him a letter to Ardkinlas, to receive him as a lost sheep; and the Colonel produces Ardkinlas's answer to that letter, dated the 9th of January 1691, bearing, "That he had endeavoured to receive the great lost sheep Glenco, and that Glenco had undertaken to bring in all his friends and followers, as the Privy-Council should order: and Ardkinlas farther writes, that he was sending to Edinburgh, that Glenco, though he had mistaken in coming to Colonel Hill to take the oath of allegiance, might yet be welcome, and that thereafter the Colonel should take care that Glenco's friends and followers may not suffer, till the king's and council's pleasure be known, as the said letter marked on the back with the letter B bears;" and Glenco's two sons above

(*Left*) Archibald Campbell, tenth Earl of Argyll, first Duke of Argyll (1701), died in 1703 (*by permission of the Duke of Buccleugh and the Duke of Argyll; photo*: National Galleries of Scotland). (*Right*) John Campbell, first Earl of Breadalbane, *c.* 1635–1717 (*photo*: National Galleries of Scotland).

Loch Triochtan, looking up the Glen with Aonach Eagach on left. To the extreme left, beyond the loch, is the site of the old hamlet of Achtriochtan (*photo: Scotsman* Publications).

Looking towards the Lairig Fhionnghail with Aonach Dubh na Glinne on the right of the pass—"Flora's Pass"—which was one of the possible escape-routes.

named, do depone in the same manner, That their father went about the end of December to Colonel Hill to take the oath of allegiance, but finding his mistake, and getting the Colonel's letter to Ardkinlas, he hasted to Inverary as soon as he could for the bad way and weather, and did not so much as go to his own house in his way to Inverary, though he past within half a mile of it, as both their depositions at the letter B. bears; and John Macdonald, the eldest son, depones farther, at the same mark, that his father was taken in his way by Captain Drummond at Barkaldin, and detained 24 hours.

Sir Colin Campbell of Ardkinlas, sheriff-depute of Argyle, depones, That the deceased Glenco came to Inverary about the beginning of January 1692, with a letter from Colonel Hill, to the effect above mentioned, and was three days there before Ardkinlas could get thither, because of bad weather; and that Glenco said to him, that he had not come sooner, because he was hindered by the storm. And Ardkinlas farther depones, That when he declined to give the oath of allegiance to Glenco, because the last of December, the time appointed for the taking, was past, Glenco begged with tears that he might be admitted to take it, and promised to bring in all his people within a short time to do the like; and if any of them refused, they should be imprisoned or sent to Flanders. Upon which Ardkinlas says, he did administer to him the oath of allegiance upon the 6th of January 1692, and sent a certificate thereof to Edinburgh, with Colonel Hill's letter, to Colin Campbell, sheriff-clerk of Argyle, who was then at Edinburgh; and further wrote to the said Colin, that he should write back to him, whether Glenco's taking of the oath was allowed by the council or not, as Ardkinlas's deposition at the letter B. testifies; and the said Colin, sheriff-clerk, depones, that the foresaid letters, and the certificate relating to Glenco, with some other certificates relating to some other persons, all upon one paper, were sent in to him to Edinburgh by Ardkinlas; which paper being produced upon oath by Sir Gilbert Elliot, clerk of the Secret Council, but rolled and scored as to Glenco's part, and his taking the oath of allegiance; yet the commissioners found that it was not so delete or dashed, but that it may be read, that Glenco did take the oath of allegiance at Inverary, the 6th day of

January 1692. And the said Colin Campbell depones, That
it came to his hand fairly written, and not dashed, and that
with this certificate he had the said letter from Ardkinlas,
(with Colonel Hill's above mentioned letter to Ardkinlas
inclosed), bearing how earnest Glenco was to take the oath of
allegiance, and that he had taken it upon the 6th of January,
but that Ardkinlas was doubtful if that the council would
receive it: and the sheriff-clerk did produce before the commissioners, the foresaid letter by Colonel Hill to Ardkinlas,
dated at Fort-William the 31st day of December 1691, and
bearing that Glenco had been with him, but slipped some
days out of ignorance, yet that it was good to bring in a lost
sheep at any time, and would be an advantage to render the
king's government easy; and with the said sheriff-clerk,
the Lord Aberuchil, Mr John Campbell, writer to the signet,
and Sir Gilbert Elliot, clerk to the council, do all declare,
that Glenco's taking the oath of allegiance with Ardkinlas,
his foresaid certificate as to his part of it, did come to Edinburgh, and was seen by then fairly written, and not scored or
dashed; but that Sir Gilbert and the other clerk of the council
refused to take it in, because done after the day appointed by
the proclamation. Whereupon the said Colin Campbell, and
Mr John Campbell, went, as they depone, to the Lord
Aberuchil, then a privy-councellor, and desired him to take
the advice of privy councellors about it: and accordingly, they
affirm, that Aberuchil said he had spoke to several privy-
councellors, and particularly to the Lord Stair; and that it
was their opinion, that the foresaid certificate could not be
received without a warrant from the king, and that it would
neither be safe to Ardkinlas, nor profitable to Glenco, to give
in the certificate to the clerk of the council; and this the Lord
Aberuchil confirms by his deposition, but doth not name
therein the Lord Stair: and Colin Campbell, the sheriff-clerk,
does farther depone, That with the knowledge of the Lord
Aberuchil, Mr John Campbell, and Mr David Moncrieff,
clerk to the council, he did by himself, or his servant, score
or delete the foresaid certificate, as now it stands scored, as
to Glenco's taking the oath of allegiance, and that he gave it
in so scored or obliterate to the said Mr David Moncrieff,
clerk of the council, who took it in as it is now produced. But

it doth not appear by all these depositions, that the matter was brought to the council board, that the council's pleasure might be known upon it, though it seems to have been intended by Ardkinlas, who both writ himself, and sent Colonel Hill's letter for to make Glenco's excuse, and desired expressly to know the council's pleasure.

After Glenco had taken the oath of allegiance, as is said, he went home to his own house, and, as his own two sons above named depone, He not only lived there for some days quietly and securely, but called his people together, and told them he had taken the oath of allegiance, and made his peace, and therefore desired and engaged them to live peaceably under King William's government, as the depositions of the said two sons, who were present, marked with the letter E, bears.

These things having preceded the slaughter which happened not to be committed until the 13th of February 1692, six weeks after the deceased Glenco had taken the oath of allegiance at Inverary. The slaughter of the Glenco-men was in this manner, viz. John and Alexander Macdonalds, sons to the deceased Glenco, depone, That Glengary's house being reduced, the forces were called back to the south, and Glenlyon, a captain of the Earl of Argyle's regiment, with Lieutenant Lindsay and Ensign Lindsay, and six score soldiers, returned to Glenco about the first of February 1692, where at their entry the elder brother John met them, with about twenty men, and demanded the reason of their coming; and Lieutenant Lindsay shewed him his orders for quartering there under Colonel Hill's hand, and gave assurance that they were only come to quarter; whereupon they were billeted in the country, and had free quarters and kind entertainment, living familiarly with the people until the 13th day of February. And Alexander farther depones, That Glenlyon being his wife's uncle, came almost every day and took his morning drink at his house; and that the very night before the slaughter, Glenlyon did play at cards in his own quarters, with both the brothers. And John depones, That old Glenco, his father, had invited Glenlyon, Lieutenant Lindsay, and Ensign Lindsay, to dine with him upon the very day the slaughter happened. But on the 13th day of February, being

Saturday, about four or five in the morning, Lieutenant Lindsay, with a party of the foresaid soldiers, came to old Glenco's house, where, having called in a friendly manner, and got in, they shot his father dead with several shots as he was rising out of his bed; and their mother having got up, and put on her clothes, the soldiers stripped her naked, and drew the rings off her fingers with their teeth; as likewise they killed one man more, and wounded another grievously at the same place. And this relation they say they had from their mother, and is confirmed by the deposition of Archibald Macdonald, indweller in Glenco; who farther depones, that Glenco was shot behind his back with two shots, one through the head, and another through the body, and two more were killed with him in that place, and a third wounded and left for dead; and this he knows, because he came that same day to Glenco's house, and saw his dead body lying before the door, with the other two that were killed, and spoke with the third that was wounded, whose name was Duncan Don, who came there occasionally with letters from the Brae of Mar.

The said John Macdonald, eldest son to the deceased Glenco, depones, The same morning that his father was killed, there came soldiers to his house before day, and called at his window, which gave him the alarm, and made him go to Innerriggen, where Glenlyon was quartered; and that he found Glenlyon and his men preparing their arms, which made the deponent ask the cause; but Glenlyon gave him only good words, and said they were to march against some of Glengaries men, and if they were ill intended, would he not have told Sandy and his niece? meaning the deponent's brother and his wife, which made the deponent go home and go again to his bed, until his servant, who hindered him to sleep, raised him; and when he rose and went out, he perceived about twenty men coming towards his house, with their bayonets fixed to their muskets; whereupon he fled to the hill, and having Auchnaion, a little village in Glenco, in view, he heard the shots wherewith Auchintriaten and four more were killed; and that he heard also the shots at Innerriggen, where Glenlyon had caused to kill nine more, as shall be hereafter declared; and this is confirmed by the concurring deposition of Alexander Macdonald, his brother, whom a

servant waked out of sleep, saying, it is no time for you to
be sleeping, when they are killing your brother at the door;
which made Alexander to flee with his brother to the hill,
where both of them heard the foresaid shots at Auchnaion
and Innerriggen. And the said John, Alexander, and Archibald Macdonalds, do all depone, That the same morning
there was one Serjeant Barber with a party at Auchnaion, and
that Auchintriaten being there in his brother's house, with
eight more sitting about the fire, the soldiers discharged
upon them about eighteen shot, which killed Auchintriaten
and four more; but the other four, whereof some were
wounded, falling down as dead, Serjeant Barber laid hold
on Auchintriaten's brother, one of the four, and asked him
if he were alive? He answered that he was, and that he desired
to die without, rather than within. Barber said, that for his
meat that he had eaten, he would do him the favour to kill
him without; but when the man was brought out, and soldiers
brought up to shoot him, he having his plaid loose, flung it
over their faces, and so escaped; and the other three broke
through the back of the house and escaped. And at Innerriggen, where Glenlyon was quartered, the soldiers took
other nine men, and did bind them hand and foot, and killed
them one by one with shot; and when Glenlyon inclined to
save a young man of about twenty years of age, one Captain
Drummond came and asked how he came to be saved, in
respect of the orders that were given; and shot him dead. And
another young boy of about 13 years, ran to Glenlyon to be
saved; he was likewise shot dead. And in the same town
there was a woman, and a boy four or five years of age killed.
And at Auchnaion, there was also a child missed, and nothing
found of him but the hand. There were likewise several killed
at other places, whereof one was an old man about 80 years
of age. And all this the deponents say they affirm, because
they heard the shot, saw the dead bodies, and had an account
from the women that were left. And Ronald Macdonald,
indweller in Glenco, farther depones, That he being living
with his father in a little town in Glenco, some of Glenlyon's
soldiers came to his father's house, the said 13th day of
February, in the morning, and dragged his father out of his
bed, and knocked him down for dead at the door; which the

deponent seeing, made his escape; and his father recovering after the soldiers were gone, got into another house; but this house was shortly burnt, and his father burnt in it; and the deponent came there after and gathered his father's bones and buried them. He also declares, That at Auchnaion, where Auchintriaten was killed, he saw the body of Auchintriaten and three more, cast out and covered with dung. And another witness of the same declares, That upon the same 13th day of February, Glenlyon and Lieutenant Lindsay, and their soldiers, did in the morning before day, fall upon the people of Glenco, when they were secure in their beds, and killed them; and he being at Innerriggen, fled with the first, but heard shots, and had two brothers killed there, with three men more and a woman, who were all buried before he came back. And all these five witnesses concur, That the foresaid slaughter was made by Glenlyon and his soldiers, after they had been quartered, and lived peaceably and friendly with the Glenco-men about 13 days, and that the number of those whom they knew to be slain were about twenty-five, and that the soldiers after the slaughter, did burn the houses, barns, and goods, and carried away a great spoil of horse, nolt, and sheep, above 1000. And James Campbell, soldier in the castle of Stirling, depones, That in January 1692, he then being a soldier in Glenlyon's company, marched with the company from Inverlochie to Glenco, where the company was quartered, and very kindly entertained for the space of fourteen days: That he knew nothing of the design of killing the Glenco-men till the morning that the slaughter was committed, at which time Glenlyon and Captain Drummond's companies were drawn out in several parties, and got orders from Glenlyon and their other officers, to shoot and kill all the countrymen they met with; and that the deponent being one of the party which was at the town where Glenlyon had his quarters, did see several men drawn out of their beds, and particularly he did see Glenlyon's own landlord shot by his order, and a young boy of about 12 years of age, who endeavoured to save himself by taking hold of Glenlyon, offering to go any where with him if he would spare his life, and was shot dead by Captain Drummond's order. And the deponent did see about eight persons killed, and several houses burnt, and women flying to the hills to save their lives. And lastly, Sir Colin Campbell of Aberuchil depones, That after the slaughter, Glenlyon told him that Macdonald of Innerriggen was killed with the rest of the Glenco-men, with Colonel Hill's pass or protection in his pocket, which a soldier brought and shewed to Glenlyon.

The testimonies above set down being more than sufficient to prove a deed so notoriously known, it is only to be remarked, that more witnesses of the actors themselves might have been found, if Glenlyon and his soldiers were not present in Flanders with Argyle's regiment: and it is farther added, that Lieutenant-Colonel Hamilton, who seems, by the orders and letters that shall be hereafter set down, to have had the particular charge of this execution, did march the night before the slaughter, with about 400 men; but the weather falling to be very bad and severe, they were forced to stay by the way, and did not get to Glenco against the next morning, as had been concerted betwixt Major Duncanson and Lieutenant-Colonel Hamilton; so that their measures being broke, Lieutenant-Colonel Hamilton, and his men came not to Glenco till about eleven of the clock after the slaughter had been committed, which proved the preservation and safety of the tribe of Glenco, since by this means the far greater part of them escaped; and then the Lieutenant-Colonel being come to Cannelochleven, appointed several parties for several posts, with orders that they should take no prisoners, but kill all the men that came in their way. Therefore some of the Lieutenant-Colonel's men marched forward in the glen, and met with Major Duncanson's party, whereof a part under Glenlyon had been sent by Lieutenant-Colonel Hamilton, to quarter there some days before, and these men told how they had killed Glenco and about 36 of his men that morning, and that there remained nothing to be done by the Lieutenant-Colonel and his men, save that they burnt some houses, and killed an old man by the Lieutenant-Colonel's orders, and brought away the spoil of the country; and this in its several parts is testified by John Forbes, major in Colonel Hill's regiment, Francis Farquhar and Gilbert Kennedy, both lieutenants in that regiment, who were all of the Lieutenant-

Colonel's party, as their depositions more fully bear.

It may be also here noticed, that some days after the slaughter of the Glenco-men was over, there came a person from —— Campbell of Balcalden, chamberlain (i.e. steward) to the Earl of Braidalbine, to the deceased Glenco's sons, and offered to them, if they would declare under their hands, that the Earl of Braidalbine was free and clear of the said slaughter, they might be assured of the Earl's kindness for procuring their remission and restitution, as was plainly deponed before the commissioners.

It remains now to give an account of the warrants, either given, or pretended to be given, for the committing of the foresaid slaughter, for clearing whereof, it is to be noticed, that the king having been pleased to offer, by proclamation, an indemnity to all the Highland rebels who should come in and accept thereof, by taking the oath of allegiance betwixt and the first of January 1692, after the day was elapsed, it was very proper to give instructions how such of the rebels as had refused his Majesty's grace should be treated; and therefore his Majesty, by his instructions of the date of the 11th of January 1692, directed to Sir Thomas Livingston, and super-signed and countersigned by himself, did indeed order and authorise Sir Thomas, "To march the troops against the rebels who had not taken the benefit of the indemnity, and to destroy them by fire and sword;" (which is the actual stile of our commissions against intercommuned rebels); but with this express mitigation in the fourth article, viz. "That the rebels may not think themselves desperate, we allow you to give terms and quarters, but in this manner only, that chieftains and heritors, or leaders, be prisoners of war, their lives only safe, and all other things in mercy, they taking the oath of allegiance; and the community taking the oath of allegiance and rendering their arms, and submitting to the government, are to have quarters and indemnity for their lives and fortunes, and to be protected from the soldiers, as the principal paper of instructions produced by Sir Thomas Livingston bears.

After these instructions, there were additional ones given by his Majesty to Sir Thomas Livingston, upon the 16th of the said month of January, supersigned and countersigned by his Majesty, and the date marked by Secretary Stair's hand, which bear orders "for giving of passes, and for receiving the submission of certain of the rebels;" wherein all to be noticed to the present purpose is, "That therein his Majesty doth judge it much better, that these who took not the benefit of the indemnity in due time, should be obliged to render upon mercy, they still taking the oath of allegiance;" and then it is added, if "Mackean of Glenco and that tribe can be well separated from the rest, it will be a proper vendication of the public justice, to extirpate that sect of thieves." And of these additional instructions, a principal duplicate was sent to Sir Thomas Livingston, and another to Colonel Hill, and were both produced; and these were all the instructions given by the king in this matter.

But Secretary Stair, who sent down these instructions, as his letters produced, written with his hand to Sir Thomas, of the same date with them, testifie, by a previous letter of the date of the 7th of the said month of January, written and subscribed by him to Sir Thomas, says, "You know, in general, that these troops posted at Inverness and Inverlochie will be ordered to take in the house of Innergarie, and to destroy entirely the country of Lochaber, Locheal's lands, Kippochs, Glengaries, and Glenco; and then adds, I assure you your power shall be full enough, and I hope the soldiers will not trouble the government with prisoners." And by another letter of the 9th of the said month of January, which is likewise before the instructions, and written to Sir Thomas, as the former, he hath this expression, "That these who remain of the rebels are not able to oppose, and their chieftains being all papists, it is well the vengeance falls there; for my part, I could have wished the Macdonalds had not divided, and I am sorry that Kippoch and Mackean of Glenco are safe;" and then afterwards, we have an account, "that Locheal, Macnaughton, Appin, and Glenco, took the benefit of the indemnity at Inverary and Kippoch, and others at Inverness." But this letter of the 11th of January, sent with the first instructions to Sir Thomas, hath this expression, "I have no great kindness to Kippoch nor Glenco, and it is well that people are in mercy, and then just now my Lord Argyle tells me, that Glenco hath not taken the oath, at which I rejoice. It is a great work of charity to be exact in rooting out that damnable sect, the worst of the Highlands." But in his letter of the 16th of January, of the same date with the additional instructions, though he writes in the first part of the letter, "The king does not at all incline to receive any after the diet, but on mercy;" yet he thereafter adds, "but for a just example of vengeance, I intreat the thieving tribe of Glenco may be rooted out to purpose." And to confirm this by his letter of the same date, sent with the other principal duplicate and additional instructions to Colonel Hill, after having written, that such as render on mercy might be saved, he adds, "I shall intreat you, that for a just vengeance and public example, the tribe of Glenco may be rooted out to purpose. The Earls of Argyle and Braidalbine have promised, that they shall have no retreat in their bounds, the passes to Ronoch would be secured, and the hazard certified to the Laird of Weems to reset them; in that case Argyle's detachment, with a party that may be posted in Island Stalker, must cut them off, and the people of Appin are none of the best."

This last letter, with the instructions for Colonel Hill, was received by Major Forbes in his name at Edinburgh, and the Major depones, That, by the allowance he had from the Colonel, he did unseal the packet, and found therein the letter and instructions as above, which he sent forward to Colonel Hill; and that in the beginning of February 1692, being in his way to Fort-William, he met some companies of Argyle's regiment at Bellisheil's, and was surprised to understand that they were going to quarter in Glenco, but said nothing till he came to Fort-William, where Colonel Hill told him, that Lieutenant-Colonel Hamilton had got orders about the affair of Glenco, and that therefore the Colonel had left it to Lieutenant-Colonel Hamilton's management, who, he apprehends, had concerted the matter with Major Duncanson. And Colonel Hill depones, That he understood that Lieutenant-Colonel Hamilton and Major Duncanson got the orders about the Glenco-men, which were sent to Lieutenant-Colonel Hamilton; that for himself, he liked not the business, but was very grieved at it; that the king's instructions of the 16th of January 1692, with the Master of Stair's letter of the same date, were brought to him by Major Forbes, who had received them, and unsealed the packet at Edinburgh, as these two depositions do bear.

Yet the execution and slaughter of the Glenco-men did not immediately take effect, and thereafter, on the 30th of the said month of January, the Master of Stair doth again write two letters, one to Sir Thomas Livingston, which bears, "I am glad Glenco did not come in within the time prefixed; I hope what is done there may be in earnest, since the rest are not in a condition to draw together help. I think to harry (that is, to drive) their cattle, and burn their houses, is but to render them desperate lawless men to rob their neighbours, but I believe you will be satisfied it were a great advantage to the nation, that thieving tribe were rooted out and cut off; it must be quietly done, otherwise they will make shift for both their men and their cattle. Argyle's detachment lies in Letrickweel to assist the garrison to do all of a sudden. And the other to Colonel Hill, which bears, "Pray when the thing concerning Glenco is resolved, let it be secret and sudden, otherwise the men will shift you, and better not meddle with them than not to do it to purpose, to cut off that nest of robbers who have fallen in the mercy of the law, now when there is force and opportunity, whereby the king's justice will be as conspicuous and useful as his clemency to others. I apprehend the storm is so great, that for some time you can do little, but so soon as possible I know you will be at work, for these false people will do nothing but as they see you in a condition to do with them."

Sir Thomas Livingston having got the king's instructions, with Secretary Stair's letter of the 16th of January, and knowing by a letter he had from the Master of Stair of the date of the 7th of January 1692, that Lieutenant-Colonel Hamilton was to be the man employed in the execution of the Glenco-men, in pursuance of the Secretary's letter, he writes to Lieutenant-Colonel Hamilton upon the 23d of the said month of January, telling him, "That it was judged good news that Glenco had not taken the oath of allegiance within the time prefixed", and that Secretary Stair in his last letter had made mention of him, and then adds, "For, Sir, here is a fair occasion for you to shew that your garrison serves for some use, and seeing that the orders are so positive from Court to me, not to spare any of them that have not timely come in, as you may see by the orders I send to your Colonel, I desire you would begin with Glenco, and spare nothing which belongs to him; but do not trouble the government with prisoners." As this letter produced by Lieutenant-Colonel Hamilton bears.

And Sir Thomas being heard upon this letter, declared, that at that time he was immediately returned from his journey to London, and that he knew nothing of any soldiers being quartered in Glenco, and only meant that he should be prosecuted as a rebel standing out, by fair hostility. And in this sense he made use of the same words and orders written to him by Secretary Stair. Thereafter Colonel Hill gives his order to be directed to Lieutenant-Colonel Hamilton, in these terms: "Sir, You are, with 400 of my regiment, and the 400 of my Lord Argyle's regiment, under the command of Major Duncanson, to march straight to Glenco, and there put in due execution the orders you have received from the commander-in-chief. Given under my hand at Fort-William, the 12th day of February 1692." And this order is also produced by Lieutenant-Colonel Hamilton.

Then the same day Lieutenant-Colonel Hamilton wrote to Major Duncanson in these terms: "Sir, Pursuant to the commander-in-chief and by Colonel's orders to me, for putting in execution the service against the rebels of Glenco, wherein you, with a party of Argyle's regiment now under your command, are to be concerned; you are therefore to order your affairs so, that you be at the several posts assigned you by seven of the clock tomorrow morning, being Saturday, and fall in action with them; at which time I will endeavour to be with the party from this place at the post appointed them. It will be necessary that the avenues minded by Lieutenant Campbell on the south side be secured, that the old fox nor none of his cubs get away: the orders are, that none be spared, nor the government troubled with prisoners." And the copy of this last order is produced under Lieutenant-Colonel Hamilton's own hand, and accordingly the slaughter of Glenco and his poor people did ensue the next morning, being the 13th of February 1692, in the manner narrated.

And upon the whole matter, it is the opinion of the com-

mission, first, that it was a great wrong that Glenco's case
and diligence, as to his taking the oath of allegiance, with
Ardkinlas's certificate of his taking the oath of allegiance on
the 6th of January 1692, and Colonel Hill's letter to Ardkinlas, and Ardkinlas's letter to Colin Campbell, sheriff-clerk,
for clearing Glencoe's diligence and innocence, were not
presented to the Lords of his Majesty's Privy-council, when
they were sent into Edinburgh in the said month of January,
and that those who advised the not presenting thereof were
in the wrong, and seem to have had a malicious design against
Glenco; and that it was a farther wrong, that the certificate as
to Glenco's taking the oath of allegiance, was delete and
obliterate after it came to Edinburgh; and that being so
obliterate, it should neither have been presented to, or taken
in by the clerk of the council, without an express warrant
from the council: secondly, that it appears to have been
known at London, and particularly to the Master of Stair,
in the month of January 1692, that Glenco had taken the oath
of allegiance, though after the day prefixed; for he saith in
his letter of the 30th of January to Sir Thomas Livingston,
as is above remarked, "I am glad that Glenco came not in
within the time prescribed:" thirdly, that there was nothing
in the king's instructions to warrant the committing of the
foresaid slaughter, even as to the thing itself, and far less as
to the manner of it, seeing all his instructions do plainly
import, that the most obstinate of the rebels might be
received into mercy, upon taking the oath of allegiance,
though the day was long before elapsed; and that he ordered
nothing concerning Glenco and his tribe, "but that, if they
could be well separated from the rest, it would be a proper
vindication of the public justice to extirpate that sect of
thieves." Which plainly intimates, that it was his Majesty's
mind, that they could not be separated from the rest of these
rebels, unless they still refused his mercy, by continuing in
arms and refusing the allegiance; and that even in that case,
they were only to be proceeded against in the way of public
justice, and no other way: fourthly, that Secretary Stair's
letters, especially that of the 11th of January 1692, in which
he rejoices to hear that Glenco had not taken the oath, and
that of the 16th of January, of the same date with the king's

additional instructions, and that of the 30th of the same month, were no ways warranted by, but quite exceeded the king's foresaid instructions, since the said letters, without any insinuation of any method to be taken that might well separate the Glenco-men from the rest, did, in place of prescribing a vindication of public justice, order them to be cut off and rooted out in earnest, and to purpose, and that suddenly, and secretly, and quietly, and all on a sudden, which are the express terms of the said letters; and comparing them and the other letters with what ensued, appear to have been the only warrant and cause of their slaughter, which in effect was a barbarous murder, perpetrated by the persons deponed against. And this is yet farther confirmed by two more of his letters, written to Colonel Hill after the slaughter was committed, viz. one on the 5th of March 1692, wherein, after having said, "That there was much talk at London, that the Glenco-men were murdered in their beds, after they had taken the allegiance," he continues, "For the last, I know nothing if it; I am sure neither you, nor any body impowered to treat or give indemnity, did give Glenco the oath; and to take it from any body else, after the diet elapsed, did import nothing at all; all that I regrate is, that any of the sort got away, and there is a necessity to prosecute them to the utmost." And another from the Hague, the last of April 1692, wherein he says, "For the people of Glenco, when you do your duty in a thing so necessary, to rid the country of thieving, you need not trouble yourself to take the pains to vindicate yourself by shewing all your orders, which are now put in the Paris gazette; when you do right you need fear nobody; all that can be said is, that in the execution it was neither so full nor so fair as might have been." And this their humble opinion, the commissioners, with all submission, return and lay before his Majesty, in discharge of the foresaid commission.

Sic subscribitur, Tweddale, Annandale, (now Marquis of Annandale, and president of the privy-council); Murray, (now Duke of Athol, and Lord Privy-Seal); James Stuart, (her Majesty's advocate); Adam Cockburn, (late Lord Treasurer Deputy;) W. Hamilton, (Lord Whitelaw, one of the Lords of the Session); Ja. Ogilvie, (now Earl of Seafield and Lord High Chancellor); A. Drummond.

Appendix XII

(See Chapter 10)

ADDRESS TO THE KING BY PARLIAMENT, COMMENTING ON THE REPORT OF THE COMMISSION

THE ADDRESS of the Noblemen, Barons, and Burroughs, in Parliament, humbly presented to His Most Sacred Majesty upon discovery communicated to them touching the murder of the Glenco-men in February 1692.

We your Majesty's most loyal and dutiful subjects, the Noblemen, Barons, and Burroughs, assembled in Parliament, do humbly represent to your Majesty that in the beginning of this session, we thought it our duty, for the more solemn and public vindication of the honour and justice of the government, to enquire into the barbarous slaughter in Glenco, February 1692, which hath made so much noise, both in this kingdom and your Majesty's other dominions; but we being informed by your Majesty's commissioner, that we awere prevented in this matter by a commission under the great seal for the same purpose, we did, upon reading of the said commission, unanimously acquiesce to your Majesty's pleasure, and returned our humble acknowledgements for your royal care in granting the same; and we only desired that the discoveries to be made should be communicated to us, to the end that we might add our zeal to your Majesty's for prosecuting such discoveries, and that, in so national a concern, the vindication might also be public, as the reproach and scandal had been; and principally that we, for whom it was most proper, might testify to the world, how clear your Majesty's justice is in all this matter.

And now your Majesty's commissioner, upon our repeated instances, communicated to us a copy of the report transmitted by the commission to your Majesty, with your Majesty's instructions, the Master of Stair's letters, the orders given by the officers, and the depositions of the witnesses relating to that report; and the same being read and compared, we could not but unanimously declare, that your Majesty's instructions, of the 7th and 16th of January 1692, touching the Highlanders who had not accepted in due time the benefit of the indemnity, did contain a warrant for mercy to all, without exception, who should offer to take the oath of allegiance, and come in upon mercy, though the 1st of January 1692, prefixed by the proclamation of indemnity, was past, and that these instructions contain no warrant for the execution of the Glenco-men made in February thereafter: and we cannot but acknowledge your Majesty's signal clemency on this occasion, as well as in the whole tract of your government over us; for had your Majesty, without new offers of mercy, given positive orders for the executing the law upon the Highlanders that had already despised your repeated indemnities, they had but met with what they justly deserved.

But it being your Majesty's mind, according to your usual clemency, still to offer them mercy, and the killing of the Glenco-men being upon that occasion unwarrantable, as well as the manner of doing it being barbarous and inhuman, we proceeded to vote the killing of them murder, and to enquire who had given occasion to it, and were the actors in it.

We found, in the first place, that the Master of Stair's letters had exceeded your Majesty's instructions towards the killing and destruction of the Glenco-men. This appeared by comparing the instructions and letters, whereof the just attested duplicates are herewith transmitted; in which letters the Glenco-men are over and over again distinguished from the rest of the Highlanders, not as the fittest subject of severity, in case they continued obstinate, and made severity necessary, according to the meaning of the instructions, but as men absolutely and positively ordered to be destroyed, without any further consideration, than that of their not having taken the indemnity in due time; and their not having taken it, is valued as a happy incident, since it

William III, King of Great Britain (1688–1702) (*photo:* National Galleries of Scotland).

John Dalrymple, Master of Stair and Secretary of State in 1692, second Viscount Stair, and first Earl of Stair (1703); died in 1707 (*from* the portrait in Oxenfoord Castle, East Lothian; *by kind permission of* the Earl of Stair).

Lairig Eilde (Pass of the Hind), one of the escape routes; between Beinn Fhada (right) and Buachaille Eite Beag (left) (*photo:* Crown Copyright, reproduced by permission of the Controller of Her Majesty's Stationery Office).

Alltnafeadh looking towards the Moor of Rannoch. The Devil's Staircase leads off to the left (*photo:* John Leng, Dundee).

afforded an opportunity to destroy them; and the destroying
of them is urged with a great deal of zeal, as a thing acceptable, and of public use; and this zeal is extended even to the
giving of directions about the manner of cutting them off;
from all which it is plain that though the instructions be for
mercy to assist all that will submit, though the day of indemnity was elapsed, yet the letters do exclude the Glenco-
men from this mercy.

In the next place, we examined the orders given by Sir
Thomas Livingstone in this matter, and were unanimously of
the opinion, that he had reasons to give such orders for cutting off the Glenco-men, upon the supposition that they had
rejected the indemnity, and without making them new offers
of mercy being a thing of itself lawful, which your Majesty
might have ordered; but it appearing that Sir Thomas was
then ignorant of the peculiar circumstances of the Glenco-
men, he might very well understand your Majesty's instructions in the restricted sense, which the Master of Stair's
letters had given them, or understand the Master of Stair's
letters to be your Majesty's additional pleasure, as it is
evident he did by the orders which he gave, where any
addition that is found in them to your Majesty's instructions,
as is given, not only to the Master of Stair's sense, but in
words.

We proceeded to examine Colonel Hill's part of the
business, and were unanimous that he was clear and free of
the slaughter of the Glenco-men; for though your Majesty's
instructions and the Master of Stair's letters were sent
straight from London to him, as well as to Sir Thomas
Livingstone, yet he, knowing the peculiar circumstances of
the Glenco-men, shunned to execute them, and gave no
orders in the matter, till such time as, knowing that his
Lieutenant-Colonel had received orders to take with him 400
men of his garrison and regiment, he, to save his own honour
and authority, gave a general order to Hamilton, his
Lieutenant-Colonel, to take the 400 men, and to put to due
execution the orders which others had given him.

Lieutenant-Colonel Hamilton's part came next to be considered; and he being required to be present, and called, and
not appearing, we ordered him to be denounced, and to be

12

seized on wherever he could be found; and having considered the orders that he received, and the orders which he said before the commission he gave, and his share in the execution, we agreed, that from what appeared, he was not clear of the murder of the Glenco-men, and there was ground to prosecute him for it.

Major Duncanson, who received orders from Hamilton, being in Flanders, as well as those to whom he gave orders, we could not see these orders, and therefore we only resolved about him, that we should address to your Majesty, either to cause him to be examined there in Flanders about the orders he received, and his knowledge of that affair, or to order him home to be prosecuted therefore, as your Majesty shall think fit.

In the last place, the depositions of the witnesses being clear, as to the share which Captain Campbell of Glenlyon, Captain Drummond, Lieutenant Lindsay, Ensign Lundie, and Sergeant Barber had in the execution of the Glenco-men, upon whom they were quartered, we agreed, that it appeared that the said persons were the actors in the slaughter of the Glenco-men under trust, and that we should address your Majesty to send them home to be prosecuted for the same according to law.

This being the state of that whole matter, as it lies before us, and which, together with the report transmitted to your Majesty by the commissioner, (and which we saw verified) gives full light to it, "WE humbly beg, that considering that the Master of Stair's excess in his letters against the Glenco-men has been the original cause of this unhappy business, and hath given occasion in a great measure to so extraordinary an execution, by the warm directions he gives about the way of surprise; and considering the station and trust he is in, and that he is absent, we do therefore beg, for the vindication of your government, as your royal wisdom shall think fit."

And likewise, considering that the actors have barbarously killed men under trust, we humbly desire your Majesty would be pleased to send the actors home, and to give orders to your advocate to prosecute them according to law, there remaining nothing else to be done for the full vindication of your government of so foul and scandalous an aspersion, as it has lain under upon this occasion.

We shall only add, that the remains of the Glenco-men who escaped the slaughter, being reduced to poverty by the depredation and vastation that was then committed upon them, and having ever since lived peaceably under your Majesty's protection, have now applied to us that we might intercede with your Majesty, that some reparation may be made for them for their losses. We do humbly lay their case before your Majesty, as worthy of your royal charity and compassion that such orders may be given for supplying them in their necessities, as your Majesty shall think fit.

And this most humble address of the Estates of Parliament, is, by their order and warrant, and in their name, subscribed by

May it please your Majesty,
    Your Majesty's most humble.
      Most obedient, and most faithful
        Subject and servant,
          ANNANDALE, P.P.
             July 10th 1695.

Appendix XIII

(See Chapter 10)

SCROLL OF DISCHARGE FROM THE KING TO STAIR

HIS Majesty considering that John, Viscount Stair, hath been employed in His Majesty's service for many years, and in several capacities, first as H.M. Advocate, and thereafter as Secretary of State, in which eminent employments persons are in danger, either by exceeding or coming short of their duty, to fall under the severities of the law, and being well satisfied that the said John, Viscount Stair, hath rendered him many faithful services, and being well assured of his affection and good intentions, and being graciously pleased to pardon, cover and secure him now after the demission of his office, and that he is divested of public employment, from all questions, prosecutions, and trouble whatsoever, and particularly, His Majesty considering the manner of the execution of the men of Glenco was contrary to the laws of humanity and hospitality, being done by these soldiers who for some days before had been quartered amongst them and entertained by them, which was a fault in the actors, or these who gave immediate orders on the place; but the said Viscount of Stair, then Secretary of State, being in London many hundreds of miles distant, he could have no knowledge of, nor accession to, the method of execution; and His Majesty being willing to pardon, forgive, and remit any excess of zeal, or going beyond his instructions by the said John, Viscount Stair, and that he had no hand in the barbarous manner of execution

Therefore His Majesty ordains a letter of remission to be made and passed his Great Seal of His Majesty's ancient kingdom, etc., and particularly any excess, crime, or fault done or committed by the said John, Viscount Stair, in the matter of Glenco, and doth exoner, pardon, indemnify and remit the said John, Viscount Stair . . . etc., etc. . . .

(Maitland Club. Papers illustrative of the Highlands— 1689–1696).

Appendix XIV

(See Chapter 10)

STORY OF CAMPBELL OF INVERAWE

THE well-known story of the ghost of Inverawe is here abridged from the version in *Selected Highland Folk-tales* by R. Macdonald-Robertson, with acknowledgements to the author.

In a private quarrel a Stewart of Appin killed Donald Campbell, brother of Duncan Campbell of Inverawe. Knowing that, as he was near Campbell country, the clan would soon be at his heels, he made for the house of Inverawe; and, relying on the ancient law of Highland hospitality whereby any man could always count himself safe while being entertained under the roof of a Highland home, received hospitality for the night. That night Duncan Campbell woke in the small hours to see with horror the pale blood-stained figure of his brother standing at the foot of his bed. "You are sheltering my murderer," said the spectre, "I demand revenge!" Campbell turned the matter over in his mind but could not bring himself to violate the time-honoured code of hospitality. On three successive nights the ghost stood at his bedside, and before vanishing for the last time, uttered a word never heard before in Argyll, "Meet me at Ticonderoga!" The injunction meant nothing to Duncan Campbell. Soon after the safe departure of Stewart from his house, Duncan joined the 42nd Highlanders with which he fought in France. Years later the Regiment was sent to America, and there they were posted to a place occupied by the French, called by the Indians "Ticonderoga". On the 17th July 1758 the 42nd attacked, and Inverawe kept the appointment made years before by the sinister figure by his bedside. It is said the ghost still haunts the now ruined old house of Inverawe.

Appendix XV

(See Chapter 9)

STORY OF CAMPBELL OF GLENLYON, GRANDSON OF ROBERT CAMPBELL OF GLENLYON OF 1692

THE following is abridged from a foot-note in the *History of the Highlands*, Vol. 2, p. 225, by James Browne, Esq., LL.D., Advocate. (The original is taken from General Stewart's *Sketches*, Vol. 1.)

Major Campbell of Glenlyon, while serving with the Marines at Havannah in 1762, was in charge of a firing party due to execute a marine for some crime. A reprieve had been sent, but the whole ceremony was to be carried through up to the last minute, when the signal was to be given by Campbell by dropping his handkerchief. No one present but Campbell himself knew of the order. As the firing party levelled their muskets, Campbell drew out the letter of reprieve, but in doing so his handkerchief too came out of his pocket and fell to the ground. The firing party carried out their orders and the marine fell. Glenlyon was aghast, and ever after regarded this as a curse falling upon him through the misdeeds of his grandfather. He shortly after retired from the Service.

Bibliography and Sources

Clan Donald, 3 Vols. Rev. Drs. Archibald and Aeneas Macdonald.

Mackenzies *History of the Macdonalds and Lords of the Isles.*

History of the Highlands, James Browne, Esq., LL.D., Advocate.

History of Scotland, Vol. VII, Hill Burton.

The Loyal Clans, Audrey Cunningham.

Claverhouse, Daviot.

Memoirs, Sir James Dalrymple.

The Annandale Family Book, Sir William Fraser, K.C.B., LL.D.

History of His Own Times, Burnet.

Famed Breadalbane, Gillies.

Memoirs, Sir Ewen Cameron of Locheil.

Jacobite Rebellions (1689–1746), J. Pringle Thomson.

The Lairds of Glenlyon, D. Campbell, 1886.

Culloden Papers.

Leven and Melville Papers.

Highland Papers, Maitland Club.

Scots Historical Review, Vol. III.

Miscellaneous Scotica (copy of B. Bragge's pamphlet, London 1704).

Tweeddale Papers.

The Loyal Dissuasive, Sir Eneas Macpherson.

Galliennus Redivivus.

The Massacre of Glencoe, John Buchan

Carmina Gadelica, Carmichael.

History of England, Macaulay.

Blackwood's Magazine, December 1847.

The Lordship of the Isles, I. F. Grant.

Highland Folkways, I. F. Grant.

Index